UK STATISTICS:
A guide for business users

UK Statistics: A guide for business users

David Mort

ASHGATE

Published by
Ashgate
Ashgate Publishing Limited
Gower House
Croft Road
Aldershot
Hants GU11 3HR
England

Ashgate Publishing Company
Old Post Road
Brookfield
Vermont 05036
USA

CIP catalogue records for this book are available from the British Library and the US Library of Congress

ISBN 0–566–02971–5

Typeset in 10pt Palatino by Photoprint, Torquay, S. Devon
Printed in Great Britain at the University Press, Cambridge

Contents

List of tables vii

Introduction 1

1. UK Published Statistics for Business 3
Currency — Methodology — Publishing — Interpretation

2. UK Published Statistics — publishing organizations and general information sources 11
Official statistics — Non-official statistics

3. Population Data 29
The population census — General population statistics — Non-official statistics: local government population data

4. Socio-economic Data 43
Classification schemes — Official statistics — Non-official statistics

5. Economic and Financial Data 67
Official statistics — The key sources — Non-official statistics — Local economic data — Alternative economic indicators — On-line databanks

6. Business Statistics 93
The Standard Industrial Classification — Official Statistics — Semi-official sources — Non-official sources

7. Labour Market Statistics 137
Official statistics — Other official sources — Non-official statistics

8. Market Research Data, Advertising and Media Information 151
Market research — Market research data — Advertising expenditure — General sources

9. Statistical Examples 173

Appendix 1. UK business statistics — contacts and addresses 183
1. Statistical publishers and services 183
2. Selected statistical libraries 195
3. General organizations and groups interested in published statistics 196

Appendix 2. Selected abbreviations and acronyms 197

Bibliography: Statistical Sources 199
General Guides and Directories — General statistics — Population statistics — Socio-economic statistics — Economic and financial statistics — Business statistics — Labour statistics — Media and advertising data

General bibliography 215

Index 219

List of tables

1.1	Selected classification schemes used for statistical purposes	7
2.1	Official statistics – general subject coverage	15
2.2	Non-official statistics – major publishers	21
3.1	Topics included in the 1991 census	32
3.2	Local areas covered by SAS	36
3.3	OPCS annual statistical titles	40
4.1	Acronyms used to classify population groups	45
4.2	Subjects covered by *Social Trends*	46
4.3	Information in the *Family Expenditure Survey*	48
4.4	Main food groups covered by the NFS	51
4.5	GHS – key topics covered continuously	52
4.6	GHS – topics included occasionally, 1971–1988	53
4.7	Subjects covered by regular CIPFA statistics	56
4.8	National opinion polls in election campaigns	57
4.9	Pinpoint identified neighbourhoods: classification summary labels	59–60
4.10	Descriptions of the 58 Mosaic postcode types	61–62
4.11	Persona behavioural types	64
5.1	Structure of the Retail Prices Index in 1991	72
5.2	CSO Press Releases – subject areas	75
5.3	Datasets on the CSO Databank	80
5.4	Bank of England Press Releases	81
5.5	Selected UK-based forecasting organizations	86
6.1	SIC (1980) revised divisions	95
6.2	UK SIC – examples of subdivisions from Division 4	95
6.3	Census of Production reports	98–100
6.4	Service sectors in *Business Monitor SDA 29*	108–109
6.5	Business Monitors not published	112
6.6	Annual sales of ceramic goods by United Kingdom manufacturers (a) PAS 2489	113

6.7	Annual sales of electronic consumer goods and miscellaneous equipment by United Kingdom manufacturers (a) PAS 3454	114
6.8	Division and section titles of the Standard International Trade Classification (Revision 3)	116–118
6.9	Example of commodity classifications and country breakdowns for product heading 882.3	119
6.10	Example of HS classification	120–121
6.11	Trade associations – key publishers of statistics	128–129
6.12	Selected UK market survey publishers	131
6.13	Some publishers of specialist market surveys	132
6.14	UK consumer markets – some company publishers	135
7.1	The Standard Occupational Classification major occupational groups	138
7.2	Regularly published statistics in the *Employment Gazette* – main subject categories	139
8.1	Joint Industry Committees	155
8.2	Market research agencies by turnover	156
8.3	Product category breakdown	164–165
8.4	MEAL statistics	166–167
8.5	Media Register statistics	168–170
9.1	Current account of the balance of payments: the 1985 balances – changing figures 1986–1990, £ million	174
9.2	GDP figures – quarterly figures, 1968–1988	175
9.3	VCR market in 1988 – a selection of the range of statistics available	178
9.4	UK export statistics and French import statistics showing the trade between UK and France in plastic syringes	180
9.5	Unemployment statistics – a comparison of LFS and figures from unemployment benefit offices (UBOs), 1984–1989	181

Introduction

The aim of this book is to provide an introduction to the range of UK published statistical sources now available to business users. It is not a comprehensive review of UK statistical publishing but a guide to key sources of information in selected subject areas of particular relevance to business users. The coverage, content, methods of collection and limitations of major titles and services in each subject area are described.

Published statistics are important sources of information for business and industry and most statistics either come from official sources, produced by central government, or non-official sources such as trade associations, professional bodies, market research organizations and economic research institutes.

In recent years, the range and nature of the published statistics available has changed significantly. The amount of official data collected and published in traditional statistical publications has been reduced in most subject areas, with one or two notable exceptions. More official statistics are now available only on demand while other official series have been passed to private sector organizations to market and distribute. The accuracy and reliability of some official series have been increasingly questioned and, in an effort to improve the statistics, changes have been made particularly in the collection and analysis of economic and business statistics. In the non-official sector, the range of statistical sources has increased dramatically. The widespread use of computer technology has also facilitated the development of more sophisticated statistical databases, such as those used in the growing area of geo-demographics. All these developments are described in the book.

Chapter 1 considers the general nature and characteristics of statistics. Chapter 2 describes the organization of statistical publishing in the UK in the 1990s and the main publishers. Chapters 3 to 8 look at statistical sources in specific subjects with individual chapters on population statistics, socio-economic data, economic and financial data, business statistics, the labour market and market research and media data.

Examples are used to show the strengths and weaknesses of statistical sources and to compare different sources. A Bibliography of all the sources mentioned is included at the end of the book and Appendix 1 gives the names and addresses of contacts for further information.

1 UK Published Statistics for Business

In 1966, an Estimates Committee report on official statistics made the observation that 'accurate, timely and relevant statistics are now generally recognised to be an integral part of the equipment with which government, industry and commerce carry out their economic tasks' (HMSO, 1966). These words are even more relevant in today's economic and business climate. The complex and often overlapping social, economic and business mechanisms of the 1990s mean that decision making, in both commercial and non-profit making organizations, is becoming more important but also more difficult. One element in good decision making is the availability of reliable information and access to accurate and up-to-date statistical data is an important part of this process.

Many organizations can generate statistical data relevant to their specific needs from within their own establishments and most organizations do so. For example, a company's sales records, a local authority's housing records, or a college's student records can provide useful indicators of the organization's general activities and performance when the data in the individual records is aggregated. For information on the social, economic and business environment in which the organization operates, it will probably be necessary to turn to external sources of information such as published statistics. In some instances, an organization might carry out its own research or commission an independent agency to carry out research specific to its needs.

With both approaches, original results should be produced which are geared specifically to the requirements of the organization but this original research can be expensive. Published statistics are unlikely to be able to provide the level of detail and uniqueness of original research but they can still offer a useful picture of a particular topic and at a significantly lower price.

The published statistics covered by this book are generally available, usually in hard copy or machine readable format, and they are produced on a regular basis, perhaps monthly, quarterly or annually. This regular supply of data creates a time series and allows the changes over a period of time to be measured. The statistics are produced by a variety of bodies in the UK but they are generally divided into 'official' and 'non-official' statistics.

'Official statistics' is the phrase used to describe all those statistics published by central government departments or a national statistical office acting on behalf of these departments. 'Non-official' sources encompasses all those statistics produced by organizations outside central government and, in this book, includes sources such as local authorities, trade associations, professional bodies, academic institutions, employers' organizations, banks and other financial institutions, private research companies, private publishers and stockbrokers.

Published statistics are still trying to live down Disraeli's famous quote of 'lies, damned lies and statistics'. Occasionally, statistics are produced using dubious methodology or are published to deliberately mislead but most statistics are collected and published in good faith.

What is true is that many statistical series have limitations and these limitations may be caused by the way in which the data have been collected, the way the results have been processed, the way the data are published, the way the statistics are used and analysed or a combination of these. An awareness of these limitations is important if published statistics are to be used effectively and specific examples of problems in the areas noted above will be given in various chapters of the book. The remainder of this chapter considers some general points about the nature and characteristics of published statistics.

Currency

Most statistics are inevitably out of date as soon as they are published because it takes time to collect, process and publish the data. In the 1950s, the then Prime Minister, Harold Macmillan, compared using government statistics to looking up train times in last year's train timetable. They usually can only tell us what has happened in the past, sometimes months or even years ago. Few statistical publications (there are exceptions such as forecasts and real-time services) tell users what they really want to know: what is happening now and what is likely to happen in the future.

Some series are published relatively quickly but then the figures are revised when more information becomes available at a later date.

Methodology

The methodology used to collect data for statistical series usually varies from one series to the next and, in turn, these differences will affect the final results. The methodology may also change over time in a specific time series making it difficult to compare figures in one series from one period with those in another period.

The majority of statistical surveys are based on samples such as a sample of consumers, a sample of companies or a sample of households. It is usually impracticable to survey the total population of people, households or companies in a given area and a sample, providing it is representative, allows information to be obtained relatively efficiently with the results being used to calculate figures for the total population.

The problem is that one sample is unlikely to be exactly the same as another. Samples are devised in different ways, response rates vary, the questions asked may differ and the answers can be obtained using different methods such as postal questionnaires, telephone interviews, face-to-face interviews, diaries and group discussions. Different methodologies mean that two surveys apparently measuring the same thing are likely to come up with slightly different results.

Some official surveys are statutory while others are voluntary and, in some instances, surveys which were originally voluntary have become statutory.

Not all statistical series are based on surveys but some are by-products of administrative systems and procedures. The monthly unemployment statistics, for example, are based on computer records of people claiming unemployment benefits. The monthly product import and export statistics come not from a special survey but from the requirement for traders to declare their imports and exports for tax and duty purposes. The product information supplied by traders to Customs and Excise is used to produce the statistics.

The advantage of using an administrative procedure to generate statistics is that the data are usually cheap and easy to collect. The disadvantages are that the statistics are influenced by any changes in the administrative procedure and the limitations of that administrative system.

The exact scope of a survey is also important with differences between surveys again producing different results. For example, a survey of sales of telephones based only on retail sales of telephones will produce quite different results from a survey based on all manufacturers' sales or a survey based on deliveries to the trade.

Definitions of what is actually being measured vary from one survey to another. This is particularly true of non-official statistics where few common definitions exist but there are also problems in comparing some official series. For example, the unemployment figures produced by the monthly count of the unemployed and those produced from the separate Labour Force Survey use different definitions of what constitutes an unemployed person.

Geographical coverage can also vary with some statistics relating to the United Kingdom, others covering Great Britain and some just concerned with England and Wales or the individual countries of the UK. Local area statistics might cover a local authority area, a health authority area or the area covered by a local TV or radio station.

Some standardization across various statistical series has been achieved through the use of a number of classification schemes. These schemes attempt to classify such things as economic activities, people, industries, products and occupations into logical categories and, usually, to describe the constituents of each category. Statistics based on these classifications can usually be compared with one another although the classifications need to be regularly updated to take account of social and economic changes.

Classification schemes appropriate to specific subject areas are described in more detail in the relevant chapters of this book but, as an introduction to the schemes and their jargon, a list of the major classifications is given in Table 1.1.

Table 1.1 Selected classification schemes used for statistical purposes

Standard Industrial Classification	(SIC)
VAT Trade Classification	(VTC)
Standard International Trade Classification	(SITC)
Harmonized Commodity Description and Coding System	(HS)
Socio-Economic Classification of the Population	
Standard Occupational Classification	(SOC)

Publishing

Most statistical data is still published in hard copy format. These statistical titles typically consist of pages and pages of tables or graphs with little or no analysis or interpretation. Usually, interpretation is left to the user which can cause its own problems as the following section shows. Most official statistics conform to this pattern, with one or two exceptions, although more non-official sources incorporate analysis and commentary.

Few statistical titles have detailed notes or explanations on how the figures have been collected although official series are usually the exception to this rule. A survey of non-official statistics in 1984 confirmed this, finding that very few sources gave detailed information on how the data had been collected (Siddall, 1984).

Once published in one source, extracts of series are then repackaged and analysed in other sources and, although this circulation of the data is generally useful, it can create problems particularly when trying to track down the exact nature and scope of the data. Many official statistics reappear in sources such as trade association reports, market research reports, on-line sources and bank and stockbroker reports.

Newspapers and trade journals also comment on official statistics and, in turn, they often include summary data from the above sources in articles and features. Figures from articles and features are then mentioned in other reports and articles. In this continual repackaging process, figures are divorced from their original context and any detailed information on the scope and nature of the data is likely to have been lost.

Interpretation

The final word is left with the user of statistics since data require effective analysis and interpretation if the information is to be useful. Any statistical series can usually be interpreted in a number of different ways while specific elements of the series can be excluded or given more weight in the final analysis. A statistical series, however well produced, can be misunderstood. There is no doubt that data can be deliberately manipulated and misinterpreted and particular statistical items excluded or emphasized to support a certain argument or point of view. In other instances, the different interpretations are genuine and result from the nature of time series data and the legitimate emphasis given to particular items in the series.

The two headlines below relate to different analyses of the same series of UK migration data published by OPCS in 1985:

MORE PEOPLE ARE ON THE MOVE (*The Times*, 29 August 1985, p. 3.)

FEWER PEOPLE ON THE MOVE (*British Business*, 6 September 1985, p. 450.)

Neither source has interpreted the data wrongly but they have each emphasized different time periods in their analysis. The *Times* article concentrated on England and Wales and compared migration trends in 1984 with trends in 1980 and 1981 when figures slumped. *British Business* compared 1984 figures with 1983 figures involving all the regions of the UK.

A more calculated example of different interpretations came in the 1987 general election campaign when the Conservative party and the Labour party both tried to score political points from the same statistics on UK Gross Domestic Product (GDP). The government argued that economic growth had averaged 2.7 per cent a year over the period 1982 to 1986 and this was true. The Labour Party took the series from 1981 to 1986 claiming that growth had averaged only 1.5 per cent a year over the seven-year period and this was also true. The government excluded the poor figures associated with the 1980–81 recession while the opposition included these in their calculations.

In some statistical series, changes in the figures in certain time periods can be caused by seasonal factors. Retail sales, for example, usually go up just before Christmas and unemployment figures can be affected by a surge of people suddenly leaving education. To smooth out these seasonal factors, many series publish seasonally adjusted figures as well as unadjusted figures. When a dual series is on offer, the figures are again open to misinterpretation and a user can deliberately opt for whichever figure suits a particular argument.

All these limitations emphasize that published statistics are not a panacea but neither do they deserve the battering they sometimes receive from their critics. Published statistics cannot provide all the answers but, if used with care, and in conjunction with other information sources, they can be effective supports to the decision-making process.

2 UK Published Statistics – publishing organizations and general information sources

Published statistics in the UK have experienced significant changes in the 1980s and early 1990s. After a gradual period of expansion up to 1979, the resources allocated to official statistical activities were reduced along with the amount of data collected and published in traditional statistical publications. More questions were also asked about the reliability and accuracy of official data.

In some areas, such as the service sector and the population census, government statistics have expanded but the greatest expansion has occurred in non-official statistics where many new titles and services have emerged. Advances in computer systems and software have helped this growth in non-official statistical services, particularly in the development of geo-demographic services and media and marketing databases. Some official series are also available on computer but too many remain unavailable in machine readable form. Specific developments and changes will be described in the subject chapters to follow.

This chapter describes the framework of statistical publishing in the UK with sections on the general organization and development of official statistics and the range and nature of non-official statistical sources.

Official statistics

Central government is the major collector and publisher of statistics in the United Kingdom and these statistics are usually referred to as official statistics. In a number of subject areas, official statistics have been collected, in one form or another, for centuries. For example, the earliest figures on the quantities and value of goods landed and discharged at ports, usually referred to as commodity import and export statistics, were collected in the thirteenth century. The first modern national population census was carried out in 1801 although William the Conqueror's 'Domesday Book' was produced long before this date.

The development of official statistics

Although a number of statistical series were well established, the government's statistical output remained largely fragmented and uncoordinated until 1941. In this year, official statistical activities were given a boost by the establishment of the Central Statistical Office (CSO) by the then Prime Minister, Winston Churchill. In subsequent years, notably in the 1950s and 1960s, there was a major expansion in the statistical output of central government, establishing the framework for the range of titles and services that exist today.

This expansion is reflected in the numbers employed in statistical activities. In 1966, over 4 200 staff worked in the government statistical service but by 1979 this total had increased by 67 per cent to just under 7 000. Expenditure on statistical activities in 1979 was £103.9 million with two-thirds of this spent on the collecting, checking and processing of data.

In the 1980s, this growth in statistical activity was halted as the resources devoted to statistical work were reduced. This change in emphasis is reflected in the number of employees in the government statistical service which fell to 6 451 in 1984 and to 4 228 by 1989.

Many of the reductions in statistical activity were initiated by the publication of the Rayner Report in 1980 which identified potential annual savings of £20 million in the provision of statistics (Rayner, 1980). The report recommended a reduction in staff to 6 100 by 1984 and an annual expenditure of £75 million (at 1979 prices).

A committee chaired by Sir Derek Rayner had looked at the collection, processing and publishing of statistics in all the major government departments as part of a wider review of Civil Service efficiency. The Rayner recommendations set the tone for the 1980s with reductions in the amount of data collected and some reduction in the amount of data published in conventional statistical publications. A greater emphasis was given to press releases, statistical bulletins and specific services on demand. The recommendations also called for an end to the subsidy of statistical publications producing increased charges for many publications and services. The effects of the Rayner review have been well documented elsewhere (Hoinville and Smith, 1982 and Siddall, 1984) but two quotes reproduced here show clearly the changing attitudes to the user of government statistics.

In 1978, Brian Mower of the CSO stated that 'the aim is to see that information is used as widely as possible . . . the great mass of information produced is there to be used by everybody. And with very few exceptions, the pricing policy is to charge only for the cost of making information available' (Mower, 1978).

By 1980, the Rayner Report noted that 'information should not be collected primarily for publication. It should be collected primarily because government needs it for its own business. We have found the CSO too heavily committed to serving the public at large' (Rayner, 1980).

Another review of government statistics was set up in 1988, concentrating particularly on statistics from the Department of Trade and Industry (Norton, 1989). The DTI study was complementary to a Cabinet Office study of inter-departmental arrangements for the production of government macro-economic statistics (HMSO, 1989). Following rumblings about the accuracy and reliability of macro-economic statistics, the Cabinet Office team recommended various ways of improving the quality of these statistics and made recommendations for organizational changes which are explained in the section titled 'The Organization of Official Statistics'.

The DTI review aimed to 'examine the arrangements for collection of economic statistics by DTI and to consider whether these procedures strike a satisfactory balance between minimizing the burdens placed on businesses providing the information required and meeting the needs for which the data are to be used by government and other customers' (Norton, 1989). The review emphasized ministerial concern about the burden imposed on companies by statistical form filling and its recommendations cut the cost to businesses of completing DTI forms by about a quarter. This was despite the fact that in a survey of 480 company data providers, carried out in the DTI study itself, only 15 per cent of respondents expressed any sort of negative attitude to filling in statistical forms. The result has been to reduce significantly the frequency and quantity of business statistics available to users (this is discussed in detail in Chapter 6).

As economic and social mechanisms become more complex, the need for accurate statistical data increases. So the general reduction in resources devoted to statistical activities, at a time of great economic and social change, created growing disquiet not only with users of official statistics but also with the providers. A government statistician, writing in the *Treasury Bulletin* in 1990, began his article with this statement: 'there is no doubt that the quality of UK economic statistics has deteriorated over the last few years' (Hibberd, 1990).

Concern amongst users was reflected in a Royal Statistical Society (RSS) report titled *Official Statistics: Counting with Confidence*, published in June 1990. Publication of the report followed an RSS meeting in December 1989 on public confidence in the integrity and validity of official statistics.

The report found no evidence of a lack of integrity in official statistics but did make a number of recommendations to 'restore confidence' in government statistics. It called for a new centralized statistical service, a new UK Statistics Act to safeguard the autonomy and constitutional position of official statistics, a new Advisory National Statistics Committee reporting annually to Parliament and bridging the gap between users and providers, and a new research unit to strengthen the methodology and evaluation of major statistical series.

Subject coverage

Official statistics have always been primarily collected to support the decision-making processes of government but the developments in statistical provision in the 1980s have served to sharpen the divide between government users and others. Official statistics naturally reflect the key interests of the national government. The result is a strong emphasis on statistics covering national and international economic and financial trends plus major statistical series on demographic trends and characteristics, the labour market, key sectors of the economy and important areas of social policy.

The problem for many business users, requiring specific data on particular sectors or products, is that the above statistics are often not disaggregated enough although some official statistics provide more

Table 2.1 Official statistics – general subject coverage

National Economic and Financial Trends
Demographic Characteristics and Projections
Labour Market Structure and Trends
Industrial Structure, Output and Performance
Product Sales and Production
Product Imports and Exports
Services and Distribution
Social Characteristics and Trends

detailed information. Data on specific products, for example, is available in the *Business Monitor* series produced by the Central Statistical Office. Surveys like the *General Household Survey* and the *Family Expenditure Survey* are also regular sources of market information providing detailed data on household characteristics and expenditure on specific goods and services.

One understandable reason why disaggregated data is not always available is that the government has an obligation not to publish data which will reveal, directly or indirectly, information about a specific company or individual.

The key subject areas covered by official statistics are listed in Table 2.1 and all these areas will be described in more detail in later chapters of the book.

The organization of official statistics

The Government Statistical Service (GSS) is the collective name given to all the statistical activities carried out by central government. The head of the GSS is also the Director of the Central Statistical Office (CSO). The CSO collects, processes and produces some government statistics but it is directly responsible for a relatively small percentage of the government's total statistical output. It produces statistical compilations like the *Annual Abstract of Statistics, Monthly Digest of Statistics, Economic Trends and Financial Statistics* plus specialist compilations such as *Social Trends* and *Regional Trends*.

Apart from these titles and various economic press releases, its main function, for over 40 years, was to co-ordinate the statistical work carried out in other government departments. Then, on 31 July 1989, its activities were expanded.

Following the 1988 review of government economic statistics (HMSO, 1989), it was decided that an enlarged CSO should have greater direct responsibility for the compilation of the national accounts and for the associated collection of data from businesses. The CSO started operating as a new government department responsible directly to the Chancellor of the Exchequer whereas previously it had been part of the Cabinet Office.

Various statistical series became the responsibility of the CSO with the aim of bringing under one management more of the work underlying the compilation of macro-economic statistics. The CSO took over the Business Statistics Office and virtually all of the statistical series for which the Department of Trade and Industry had been responsible, including the overseas trade figures. The retail prices index, which had previously been the responsibility of the Department of Employment, also transferred to the CSO. In November 1991, the CSO also became one of the new executive style agencies.

The CSO now has a much more central role in the preparation of macro-economic statistics. The vast majority of government statistical work remains decentralized with individual government departments responsible for statistics relevant to their areas of interest. Within a department the majority of statisticians are located in a central statistical division headed by an under secretary or even a deputy secretary.

Two specialist statistical agencies cover topics of particular importance. The CSO's office at Newport, previously known as the Business Statistics Office (BSO), covers business statistics and the Office of Population Censuses & Surveys (OPCS), with its main offices in London, covers population statistics.

Along with the CSO and OPCS, there are 14 major departments collecting and producing statistical data. Publications from most of these departments will be mentioned in the following chapters of the book. They are, in alphabetical order:

Board of Inland Revenue
Department of Education & Science (DES)
Department of Employment
Department of the Environment (DOE)
Department of Health

Department of Trade and Industry (DTI)
Department of Transport
HM Customs & Excise
HM Treasury
Home Office
Ministry of Agriculture, Fisheries & Food (MAFF)
Northern Ireland Departments
Scottish Office
Welsh Office

A selection of other government departments and agencies involved to a lesser extent in statistical work include the following:

Department of National Savings
Government Actuary's Department
Health & Safety Executive
Lord Chancellor's Department
Meteorological Office
Ministry of Defence
Office of Fair Trading
Office of Manpower Economics
Overseas Development Administration
Registry of Friendly Societies
Scottish Education Department
Scottish Health Service

This decentralized approach to statistical work is not common. Most other developed countries prefer a centralized statistical office responsible for most of the national statistical work.

A decentralized system is based on the principle that a department responsible for collecting statistical information is the best placed to define, publish and answer for any published statistics produced. It should also facilitate a more effective use of the data within government as statisticians work more closely with decision makers and policy administrators in specific departments.

One drawback of the system is that departments leave themselves open to the accusation that they can massage or change the way data is collected or presented in order to suit their policy objectives. This approach also means that the priority given to statistical work and the quality and coverage of the statistics themselves can vary considerably from department to department. It may also create divided loyalties as statisticians have responsibilities to the statistical service as a whole and also their particular line managers in specific departments.

For the outside user of government statistics, the lack of a central unit responsible for all published data can be confusing. Many occasional users assume that the CSO is the only government office responsible for government statistics. Even regular users can find it frustrating and time consuming tracking down the right department and person responsible for a particular statistical series. How many outside users, for example, would automatically appreciate that official statistics on tourism are published by the Department of Employment?

The strength of official statistics is that the methods of compilation and definitions used are open to public scrutiny and debate. The widespread debate and discussion accompanying the various changes to the way in which the unemployment figures were collected in the 1980s provides the clearest example of this. For important surveys, such as the ten-yearly population census, and in major subject areas, there are regular consultations and meetings with interested groups and parties.

For specific users, all government statistical publications have notes describing the methods of compilation and definitions used although sometimes these are published as part of the statistical publication, sometimes separately and sometimes they are only available on request from the producing department. Individual statisticians responsible for specific series can also be identified to provide further information and help.

Official statistical publications and services

Most regular official statistical series are published in conventional statistical titles made up largely of tables and, sometimes, graphs and charts. Very few publications include any analysis or interpretation of the data although there are one or two exceptions such as *Social Trends* and the *General Household Survey*.

Most of the statistical titles, like other official publications, are available through HMSO. These can be ordered from the central HMSO Publications Centre or through the various HMSO bookshops around the country. The shops normally stock the general statistical compilations produced by CSO but other titles on specific subject areas will need to be ordered.

While HMSO publishes the bulk of official statistics, it is by no means responsible for everything with individual departments also publishing titles. Departmental publishing has increased since the Rayner Report following its recommendation that more statistics should be published in the form of press releases and statistical bulletins.

Statistical Bulletins appear regularly throughout the year and usually provide timely statistics on specific topics on two or three sheets of paper. They have become popular publications in many departments but particularly at the Department of Transport, Department of Education, Home Office and the Department of the Environment. OPCS also publishes a series of *Monitors* on specific population topics. These publications must be ordered direct from the relevant departments, as must the selection of other publications which bypass HMSO.

The dual publishing arms of HMSO and specific departments can be another source of confusion to the user. For example, the annual *Digest of UK Energy Statistics* is published through HMSO but the monthly *Energy Trends*, which updates some of the basic data in the annual, is only available direct from the Department of Energy. Until recently, Welsh Office statistical publications were available from HMSO but now they must be purchased direct from the Welsh Office in Cardiff.

As the amount of data published in conventional statistical compilations declines, more and more of the detailed statistical output is available only in specific packages and services. These services are usually available on request, and for a fee, from individual departments and are produced in a variety of formats including fiche, magnetic tape, discs and computer printouts. The published statistical volumes usually give contact names and addresses for users requiring more detailed information.

Users should also check non-statistical publications and sources for statistics. For example, written answers to parliamentary questions often incorporate statistical data and tables and these answers are reported in *Hansard*. Statistics also appear in annual reports and reviews from government departments and agencies.

On-line access to official statistics is growing very slowly and the coverage remains patchy. The CSO's *Databank*, covering basically macro-economic time series, is available via a number of commercial hosts as are detailed import and export data, some labour market statistics and population data, but other areas of official statistics have failed to appear in on-line form. Sadly, plans to develop an on-line database covering the product statistics published in the *Business Monitor* series appear to have stalled.

Major official statistical series, such as population census and census of employment data, and statistics from regular surveys like the General Household Survey and Family Expenditure Survey are deposited at the ESRC Data Archive. The Archive, founded in 1967 by the University of Essex and the then Social Science Research Council, holds and disseminates data collected by social investigators from the public and private sectors and there are plans to extend the range of official data deposited here. Prospective users can contact the Archive for a specialized search of data holdings related to a particular area of interest and further details are given in the Appendix.

A quick, useful source of information on official statistics is the annual CSO publication, *Government Statistics – a brief guide to sources*. This lists the major official statistical titles but also includes a list of departmental responsibilities and contact points with telephone numbers for information on specific statistical series. The publication is free and supplements the less frequent, but more detailed, *Guide to Official Statistics,* published every few years by HMSO. The 6th edition was published in 1990 and follows previous issues in 1986, 1982, 1980, 1978 and 1976.

The guide is arranged in subject sections and aims to cover all official and some important non-official sources of statistics giving general descriptions of relevant publications. Ad hoc reports and articles are covered in addition to regular statistical titles. It also lists government department contact points.

The guide offers the most comprehensive description of official statistics but it should be used with care and not treated as a detailed index to sources of data. Although a general subject index is included in the guide, it does not always positively identify a source for particular detailed statistics: in some cases, it may only indicate that a certain publication probably contains the required information. For example, the *General Household Survey* includes data on household ownership of video recorders but there is no index entry for these in the Guide and the description of the publication only mentions the general term 'consumer durables'. The only satisfactory way to find out if the data on video recorders exists is to consult the *General Household Survey* itself.

For statistics published by individual departments a regular source is the *Catalogue of British Official Publications not Published by HMSO,* published 6 times a year by Chadwyck-Healey Ltd. This lists all

Table 2.2 Non-official statistics – major publishers

Trade Associations
Professional Organizations
Local Authorities and other Local Organizations
Market Research and Market Survey Companies
Media Organizations
Financial Institutions
Stockbrokers
Economic Research Institutes
Trade Journal Publishers
Manufacturing Companies
Academic Institutions

departmental publications, statistical and non-statistical, produced in the previous two months and includes a general subject index. An annual volume is also produced. Chadwyck-Healey can supply fiche copies of most of the documents listed in the catalogue.

Statistical News is a quarterly bulletin produced by CSO with feature articles and news items covering statistical developments. One section gives details of new surveys deposited at the ESRC Data Archive.

Non-official statistics

When official statistics are unable to give sufficient detail it may be that non-official sources can provide the answer.

Key publishing organizations

Non-official statistics are published by various organizations outside central government and they often cover specific products, markets, industries and geographical areas in much more detail than official sources. A list of the major publishers of non-official statistics is given in Table 2.2.

Trade associations

Trade associations are the major producers of regular statistics outside central government. There are over 6 000 trade associations in the United Kingdom representing and working on behalf of member companies usually in a specific industry or sector. Many of these carry out no statistical functions at all but the *Directory of British Associations* published by CBD Research lists 1 300 trade associations involved in statistical activities. Of these 1 300, only between 400 and 500 publish statistics on their area of interest on a regular basis.

There is no typical example of a trade association with the number of members, resources and types and levels of services varying from one association to another. Some associations, like the Society of Motor Manufacturers and Traders and the British Paper and Board Industry Federation, have been around since the beginning of the century but others, like the British Videogram Association, have only been established recently. Some associations have merged while others have split up to form other associations as specific sectors of an industry have become more important. Associations can cover very small product or industry sectors while others represent the interests of large sectors such as the engineering or chemicals industry.

The statistical output from trade associations reflects the fact that they are not a homogeneous group and the accuracy and reliability of the data can vary considerably from one association to another. Some trade association statistics are excellent while others should be treated with caution!

Many trade associations simply repackage and comment on official statistics but, in the absence of any interpretation of the data from official statisticians, these associations provide a useful function which fills an information gap. A number of associations, for example, publish product sales and import and export data, often with a commentary, based on data originally published in official sources.

Other associations are publishing original data usually based on a survey of their member companies or a sample of their members. If an association has a significant proportion of the companies in the industry in its membership then the figures should be reliable. Figures based on only a small percentage of companies in the industry, or missing responses from the leading companies, will not be so accurate.

Accessing trade association data can sometimes be problematic since few libraries or on-line services cover many of the statistics, particularly those from the smaller associations. Confidentiality is also a problem with some associations providing the data to their member companies only. As associations are there primarily to serve their members, and are mostly funded by them, these restrictions are hardly surprising although the amount of information restricted is not as great as might be imagined.

A survey of non-official statistics by Warwick University (Siddall, 1984) found that 41 per cent of trade association titles were restricted to members only with the majority available generally. Even where detailed statistics are limited to member companies, some associations provide summary data or older data to other inquirers.

Professional organizations

Probably the single major publisher of statistics outside central government is a professional body, the Chartered Institute of Public Finance and Accountancy (CIPFA). CIPFA publishes a series of regular titles on local government and public sector finance and services and these are described in Chapter 4. Many other professional bodies publish statistics which typically look at the characteristics and activities of their members, usually individual professionals. Surveys of employment and salary characteristics and trends are the most common and these are described briefly in Chapter 7.

Local authorities and other local organizations

There are 536 local authorities around the United Kingdom. All of these are potential sources of statistical data, although, in reality many of these will publish very little. Despite this, an estimated 50 000 reports and surveys are produced by local authorities each year and many of these contain statistical data. Local authority publications are often considered as official publications but in this book they are treated as non-official sources to differentiate them from central government statistics.

Apart from published data, authorities can obtain detailed statistics from central government relating to their areas. For example, local government can purchase detailed local Census of Employment data under the Town and Country Planning Act 1973. Some of this data may be repackaged and published in a local government publication although, in the above example, it is necessary to obtain permission for the publication.

Other authorities have established their own statistical and information units carrying out original statistical surveys and studies although the number of these is still relatively small. This lack of local authority based statistical services was noted in an article in 1990 (Worral, 1990) when the author stated 'one would expect that the poor quality of nationally available statistical series would have prompted local government to develop systems to support policy analysis and development: this has generally not been the case'. Cost-cutting, the absence of people with the necessary vision and skills and the need to apply valuable resources to coping with the impact of central government imposed legislation are given as the causes of the lack of an original extensive statistical base in local government.

The abolition of the metropolitan counties also removed some of the larger statistical and information units around the country although, in a number of areas, other units have been established in their place. For example, there is the London Research Centre and in the north west, the Greater Manchester Research and Information Planning Unit (GRIPU) and the Merseyside Information Service. These units are usually funded by a number of local authorities in a particular locality.

Other information services have been developed by groups of authorities in a particular region to look at areas of common interest. Examples include the London and South East Regional Planning Conference (SERPLAN) and the East Anglia Consultative Committee.

As for the publications themselves, a few authorities publish regular statistical compilations or bulletins perhaps appearing annually or, in other cases, quarterly or even monthly. County councils publish an annual report covering their activities and services and most of these contain statistical data. Other local authority documents containing statistics include policy papers, planning documents, research studies and papers, committee papers and inquiry reports. Most reports relate to the areas covered by local authority services. Popular subject areas are population trends and projections, housing, employment, unemployment, transportation, construction and industrial development.

The major problem for users of these statistics is that tracking them down can be a time consuming and frustrating business. There are usually many departments publishing documents and few authorities have a central publishing unit which can deal with requests from outside users. Many publications have small print runs and are only distributed to interested parties in the local area. Very few titles are covered by the general abstracting publications or services.

Other local organizations involved in statistical publishing include chambers of commerce, development agencies and enterprise boards.

Market research and market survey companies

Market research reports and services can come in various forms. First, there are those companies, usually known as 'market survey' organizations, which bring together mainly existing sources of data in one report with a commentary, analysis and interpretation. Many of these are one-off reports, or they are only published at irregular intervals, so they are not covered by this book.

Other organizations provide original data based on field research techniques. Some of this data appears in one-off reports or commissioned reports for specific clients but other services are available at regular intervals or continuously. These include omnibus surveys, retail audits, store checks and opinion polls. Most of these continuous surveys relate to consumer markets with the large companies such as Nielsen and AGB offering a range of services and smaller companies specializing in specific product and market areas. On-line access to market research data is well developed and this is discussed in Chapter 8.

Media organizations

The Advertising Association publishes statistics on general advertising trends while two specialist services, Media Expenditure Analysis Ltd (MEAL) and the Media Register, provide regular data on brands, advertisers, advertising medium etc. There are a number of obstacles to producing a comprehensive picture of advertising expenditure and these are considered in more detail in Chapter 8.

Viewing, listening and readership habits are measured in various surveys, available in published and machine readable form, and most of the independent TV companies publish regular statistical compilations on their area.

Financial institutions

The Bank of England and the International Council of the Stock Exchange are regular statistical publishers and all the major clearing banks publish economic data and, in some cases, industry statistics. Other financial sectors covered include building societies, the housing market and house prices, insurance, credit and unit trusts.

Stockbrokers

Regular analyses of industry sectors are produced by research departments of stockbrokers although most of these reports concentrate on company information. Some reports are only available to client companies while other stockbrokers are willing to sell or give their reports to a wider audience.

Economic research institutes

Various economic research institutes, both private and public, are involved in the analysis of economic data and the preparation of economic and industry forecasts.

Trade journal publishers

Trade journals are an often underestimated source of statistical data. Some journals have regular statistical sections often reproducing and summarizing statistics from other sources such as trade associations, market research companies and official statistics. Others collect and publish their own statistics or commission a survey from a market research company. Annual reviews of specific market sectors appear in a number of journals, sometimes published as a supplement to the regular journal issue.

Manufacturing companies

Although largely intended as publicity or branding exercises, market reports and reviews published by private companies can contain useful data. The reports, usually available free from the company or its public relations agency, are often based on original research commissioned by the company. Many UK-based companies, particularly in the food and drink sector, publish regular reviews and further details are given in Chapter 6.

Academic institutions

A selection of departments in universities and polytechnics now publish regular statistical reviews often based on the research being carried out in these departments. Economic and business reviews are common plus bulletins on specific sectors such as agriculture and textiles.

Non-official statistics – strengths and weaknesses

The main advantage of non-official statistics are that they can provide more detailed information on specific business sectors and they cover many products and sectors excluded from central government data.

They also include different types of data. For example, official statistics on products concentrate on total sales or production figures but non-official sources might cover other areas such as trade deliveries, stocks, end-users, retail sales, sales by geographical area, sales by type of outlet and forecasts.

Particular types of surveys such as salary surveys, opinion polls and trend surveys are almost exclusively produced by non-official organizations. Non-official sources are usually the first to cover new product and service areas and may be the first to react to changes in specific sectors.

The main disadvantage of non-official statistics stems from the fact that the data comes from all shapes and sizes of organizations with different interests plus different levels of statistical expertise and resources. In this environment, judging the accuracy and reliability of a particular source can be difficult particularly as, unlike official statistics, few sources give any details about how the figures have been compiled.

Publishing and marketing trends also vary from organization to organization. Non-official statistics sometimes appear in standard statistical publications but they are also produced in annual reports, press releases, yearbooks, journals, monographs or on two sheets of A4 paper photocopied and stapled together!

Some publishers, notably market research companies and some trade associations, have an extensive range of publications and services which are marketed and sold to as wide an audience as possible. Other publishers, including some trade associations, local authorities and stockbrokers, have no desire to reach a wider audience or fail to see the wider value of their information.

In these circumstances, and given the fact that much of the information produced relates to very specific sectors and products, it comes as no suprise to find that few libraries have extensive holdings of non-official data. For the same reasons, very little non-official data has appeared on on-line databases although market research and advertising data is an exception.

Non-official statistics – sources of information

There are few bibliographies and guides covering the complete range of non-official sources but guides and indexes covering specific types of information or organizations, such as MSI's monthly *Marketing Surveys Index* or CBD's *Directory of British Associations* can help (see Appendix for further details). One specific guide to non-official sources is *Sources of Unofficial UK Statistics*, published by Gower and listing and describing over 1 000 publications. There is a subject index to the entries and a title index. The *Directory of Business Information Sources* published by Macmillan lists the main official and non-official sources, by UK SIC sectors.

3 Population Data

Reliable measures of changes in the size and characteristics of the population are vital if social and community planning and policies are to be effective. Central and local government use population indicators and projections as policy aids in various areas including health, housing, transport, education, social services, community planning and leisure and recreation. Many businesses use population data, at a national and local level, to measure potential markets and market segments.

In recognition of the importance of population statistics, a specialist statistical unit within central government, the Office of Population Censuses and Surveys (OPCS), has been established to collect and distribute demographic data. OPCS is responsible for numerous weekly, monthly, quarterly and annual population publications and most of these are described in this chapter.

At the centre of the range of statistics is the population census which is currently undertaken every ten years. The census is the most extensive statistical survey in the country giving comprehensive data on the characteristics of the population both at a national and local level. Local authorities can also supply population data at a local level, sometimes repackaging central government data and, in other cases, carrying out their own original surveys.

The population census

The most comprehensive source of population data is the population census. This is one of the few statistical surveys that is based on a 100 per cent sample: census questionnaires are delivered to every household and communal establishment. The results are processed, not only at a national level, but for small geographical areas and small groups on a unified basis across the country. This ability to provide data for small areas or small population groups is what makes the population census unique.

Information is collected on individual households but this information is confidential and only aggregate data is published. Census information on individuals and individual households remains confidential for 100 years and then the individual census forms are released.

One of the first examples of a census in this country was the Domesday survey, ordered by William the Conqueror, which provided a detailed description of the population in Norman England. The latest census took place on Sunday, 21 April 1991 and was the twentieth in the current series of censuses which began in 1801. Census questionnaires were sent to 24 million households and the cost of the exercise is estimated at £135 million over a ten-year period.

A full census has been held every ten years since 1801, except in 1941, although a national register of the population was produced in 1939. A sample census was also carried out in 1966. The next census is likely to be in 2001 although there may be a sample census in 1996. A 1996 survey is unlikely but any decision on this must be taken by the end of 1992 because of the necessary lead-in times required.

The 1841 census is usually seen as the first modern census because, for the first time, households were asked to complete the census form themselves and their names and addresses were recorded. In earlier years, enumerators visited households to obtain summary data and this data was then aggregated to provide a total picture.

The census offers the longest time-series of demographic and social statistics in Britain although comparing the results from one census to another can be difficult, particularly on specific topics, as questions and definitions change along with other variables such as local government boundaries. For example, nine questions from the 1971 census were not included in the 1981 census and one question –

whereabouts on census night of each person entered on the household form – appeared for the first time in 1981.

A detailed description of the history of the census from 1801 to 1966 is given in *A Guide to Census Reports 1801–1966* (HMSO, 1977) and some of the problems associated with using census data are outlined in *Secondary Analysis in Social Research; A Guide to Data Sources and Methods* (Hakim, 1982).

In England and Wales, the census is carried out by the Office of Population Censuses and Surveys (OPCS) and hundreds of temporary staff are brought in to deal with this vast statistical exercise. Separate censuses for Scotland and Northern Ireland are the responsibility of the General Register Offices (GROs) in Edinburgh and Belfast respectively. Jersey has had its own census since 1821 with the latest in March 1991. From 1961, Guernsey has carried out its own census and these have been quinquennial since 1971.

Planning for the next census begins immediately after the last census has been completed and there is extensive consultation and debate on the need for a census, the topics to be included and the form that the census should take. The proposed questions and methods of collecting and processing the data are tested in census tests in sample geographical areas around the country.

Plans for the 1991 census were announced in the *White Paper; 1991 Census of Population* published in July 1988 and census tests were carried out in 1987 and 1989. In 1990, confirmation that the 1991 census would take place appeared in the *Census Order* which described the questions to be included in the census form. The majority of questions in 1991 could be answered by simply ticking a box and most households were expected to complete the form in under 30 minutes.

Census information

The census is not just a count of the population; it provides data on a range of topics including detailed demographic characteristics; employment, unemployment, occupation and working hours; education; housing; migration; amenities; travel and transport; and health. The extent of its coverage can be seen by the topics included in the 1991 census, listed in Table 3.1.

The Northern Ireland census excludes the question on ethnic group but it has an additional question on religion which is answered on a voluntary basis. There is also a question on the Irish language. In Guernsey, the topics are slightly different. For example, there are no

Table 3.1 Topics included in the 1991 census

Household topics

* Type of accommodation
* Tenure
* Number of rooms
* Bathroom and WC
* Central heating
* Number of cars or vans
* Lowest floor level of accommodation (Scotland only)

Personal topics

* Name
* Address of enumeration
* Usual address
* Sex
* Date of birth
* Marital status
* Relationship in household
* Country of birth
* Scottish Gaelic language (Scotland only)
* Welsh language (Wales only)
* Ethnic group
* Address one year ago
* Term-time address of students
* Economic position/employment status
* Occupation
* Industry of occupation
* Hours worked weekly
* Address of workplace
* Means of travel to work
* Higher education qualifications
* Long-term illness

questions on long-term illness but other questions on migration, country of birth (because of the island's large migratory population), health insurance and second occupations.

Many topics have been included in every census but others are relatively new, or may only appear once. A question on car ownership was included in the sample 1966 census, reflecting the dramatic growth in car ownership in that period, and a question on this topic has appeared in every census since. As home ownership rose, the household tenure question was introduced in 1961 and is still there. All the topics covered by the 1981 census were included in the 1991 census but five new questions were introduced. These new questions covered ethnic group, the term-time address of students, hours worked weekly, long-term illness and central heating.

Published output

The census produces a great deal of useful data but the sheer volume of statistics generated can cause basic problems for the potential user. First, it is necessary to track down what is available and how it is available. Various national, local and topic reports form the bulk of the published output from the census but more detailed statistics are available in other formats such as microfiche, discs and computer print-out.

Only a small percentage is actually published in traditional hard copy reports and a significant amount of the detailed statistics can only be obtained by requesting it specifically from OPCS. In the 1971 census, for example, the total output amounted to 1.6 million pages of tables but only 38 000, or 2.3 per cent, were available in standard published volumes. In the 1981 census, the aim was to reduce the amount of published pages to 20 000.

Secondly, processing and analysing the vast amount of data collected takes time. In the past, a major problem for users has been the delay in publishing results. Speed of publication in the 1981 census was much improved over 1971 and further improvements were anticipated in the 1991 census. However, as this book was being completed at the beginning of 1992, publication of 1991 census results was well behind the original planned schedule. Preliminary results were published in Summer 1991 and other results will be published from June 1992 onwards.

Thirdly, not all published statistics are based on a 100 per cent sample of responses. Where specific questions can be relatively easily analysed and processed, the published data is based on a 100 per cent sample but where the processing and analysing of all the results is likely to be difficult, the published results are only based on a 10 per cent sample. In the 1991 census, published results from a 10 per cent sample cover the following topics: relationship in household;

occupation; industry of occupation; hours worked weekly; address of workplace; means of travel to work; and higher education qualifications.

The following section describes some of the publications and services available from the census concentrating on OPCS with some additional comments on Scottish and Northern Ireland publications.

The first results from the census are published a few months after the census date in a series of pamphlets titled *County Monitors*. Each monitor gives a preliminary count of the population in a specific county with additional data on sex and age structure. The statistics cover the county as a whole and the individual local authority areas within each county.

A few months later, detailed statistics on each county area are published in a series of *County Reports*. These are published in two volumes covering all the major census variables and they include county-wide data and data on specific local authority areas. The first volume has statistics based on a 100 per cent sample and the second volume contains statistics based on a 10 per cent sample.

In Scotland, preliminary results are published in a series of *Regional Monitors*, with information on the region as a whole and local authority areas within the region, followed by a series of *Regional Reports* with more detailed information. In the 1981 census, these regional reports were published in four volumes per region.

National Report: Great Britain is a two-volume report which brings together the main census variables included in the above reports. Other similar reports are published for Scotland, Wales and Northern Ireland.

A problem for census users is that the county and regional reports described above are not published at the same time. Instead, they appear gradually over a period of time reflecting the order in which data on the individual counties and regions have been processed. This can be frustrating for users who may have the Isle of Wight report in front of them but then might have to wait months before a similar report on another county, such as Staffordshire, becomes available.

Counties are processed in a particular order to take account of various requirements. For example, faster growing counties are usually given priority over other areas. Counties with a significant number of armed forces personnel are given a higher priority in order to advance the results for population estimates purposes. At least one county from each standard region in England and Wales is processed relatively early. The processing order also reflects the production order requested by the Department of the Environment and the Scottish and Welsh Offices.

Finally, the processing schedule aims to balance the workload of the separate processing streams and to start with relatively straightforward counties with fewer numbers of district authorities and no expected boundary changes. All these requirements mean that, although the first county reports from the 1991 census were published in Summer 1992, it will probably be 1993 before the last reports on the list are published.

New reports which appeared for the first time in the 1981 census present general census data for geographical areas other than the standard local authorities. A set of Monitors, for example, presents summary statistics for parliamentary constituencies and another set gives similar data for wards and parishes. The new town areas in England, Wales and Scotland are covered by separate reports.

As well as general reports, census reports are also published on individual topics and usually these reports give national data and local data down to county level. Subjects covered by individual topic volumes from the 1991 census include: ethnic group and country of birth; long-term illness; sex, age and marital status; migration; workplace and transport to work; housing; household composition; communal establishments; economic activity; qualified manpower. The first topic volume is scheduled for publication in September 1992 with the last title likely to appear at the end of 1993.

While information at county and local authority level is useful, many users of the census need even more detailed local data and this is provided in a two-tier set of standard statistical tables for local areas. The upper tier, called the local base statistics, is available for local government districts and wards, and also for postcode sectors in Scotland. The lower tier are known as Small Area Statistics (SAS) which are census statistics arranged by Enumeration Districts, usually referred to as EDs.

The ED is the basic administrative unit for the census and an ED area typically contains 175 to 225 households. Over the whole country, there are approximately 130 000 EDs. When planning the census, the local government district area is used as the basic working unit and, within these districts, EDs are planned on a ward by ward basis.

SAS for specific EDs are not published in conventional hard copy reports but they are available on magnetic tape. In Scotland, the SAS

Table 3.2 Local areas covered by SAS

'Low levels':

Enumeration Districts
Civil Parishes (Communities in Wales)
Wards
London Boroughs
Local Authority Districts
Counties (Regions & Island Authorities in Scotland)
Regional Health Authorities
District Health Authorities
Postcode Sectors

Additional areas in Scotland:

Regional Electoral Divisions
Localities
Parliamentary Constituencies
Inhabited Islands
New Towns
Health Boards

'High levels' in England and Wales:

National Levels
Standard Regions in England
Parliamentary Constituencies
European Constituencies
Urban/Rural Areas

are based on postcodes and SAS are available for specific 'output areas'. SAS are also available for a range of other local areas and the areas available are listed in Table 3.2. The first 100 per cent local base statistics and SAS were available in 1992.

Included on the census questionnaire is the postcode of the address on census night. Information on the postcode has been obtained in earlier censuses but never put into the computer, except in Scotland. For the first time in 1991, postcodes are being put into the census computer and this will enable statistics to be produced for postcode areas. SAS for postcode sectors will be available after the main SAS programme is completed from October 1992 onwards. There are also plans to produce SAS for customized small areas built up from specified aggregates of postcodes. These would be available from 1992 onwards.

Although individual questionnaire records from the census remain confidential for 100 years, two sets of 'samples of anonymized records' (SARs) are likely to be released from the 1991 census. These would complement the information available from the traditional type of tabulated census statistics.

This innovation follows a request from the Economic and Social Research Council (ESRC) and it will allow users to assess which extra tables it would be cost effective to commission from the full census details. One of the samples will be of individuals and the other will cover households. Census users can also commission special tables and these will start to become available from the third quarter of 1992.

Finally, census information is repackaged and analysed in various other publications and services from local authorities, economic research organizations, academic institutions and the geodemographic research services produced by commercial organizations. These latter services are described in more detail in Chapter 4. Local authority data is considered in more detail in this chapter.

General population statistics

In between the ten-yearly census, OPCS produces other measures of the population which appear on a regular basis, annually, quarterly, monthly or even weekly. Many of these statistics are published as part of the *OPCS Monitor* series, which includes various titles on specific population topics.

Population estimates

OPCS Monitor PP1, Population Estimates for England and Wales is an annual publication which uses the census population data as the base figure and then gives mid-year population estimates nationally and by regions, counties, local authority districts, local boroughs and health authority areas. Similar publications for Scotland and Northern Ireland are published by the respective GROs. More detailed information is available on floppy disc.

The estimates include all residents of whatever nationality and the annual update takes into account births, deaths and migration plus changes in the armed forces and dependents, and prisoners. These annual figures can only be estimates since a complete count of the total population is not feasible.

The main problem in calculating the figures stems from the measurement of migration. Various sources are used to calculate migration trends. International migration figures come from the International Passenger Survey which is based on a sample of the passengers moving through ports and airports. Migration within the UK is calculated from two sources – the National Health Service Central Register (and its equivalents in Scotland and Ireland), and changes in the numbers on local electoral rolls, although both these sources are unlikely to give a comprehensive picture.

Figures are collected by OPCS and the GRO (in Scotland and Northern Ireland) from local electoral registration offices in February or March each year. Only persons aged 18 and over are included and only UK, Commonwealth or Republic of Ireland citizens are on it.

Householders are obliged by law to supply data for the Electoral Register but there are wide variations from area to area in response rates. In 60 per cent of local authorities, 95 per cent of households or more respond to the request for information but, in 4 per cent of authorities, the response is lower than 80 per cent. It is particularly low in a number of London boroughs but very high in non-metropolitan districts.

Registration usually increases as a general election approaches while changes in legislation can push registration upwards or downwards. The arrival of the community charge, for example, pushed registration downwards.

Since 1951, the National Health Service Central Register has been maintained by OPCS at its offices in Southport. The register is used mainly to help Family Health Service Authorities, previously called Family Practitioner Committees, to maintain lists of patients for doctors, to control the issue of NHS numbers and to ensure the transfer of medical records when people move.

Its information on internal migration, based on patients changing from one doctor to another, is used in the production of the population estimates although again it has limitations: for example, persons moving areas may not register immediately with a new doctor or may not register at all.

Population projections

Population projections show what the population would be in the future. These projections are based on various assumptions concerning fertility, birth rates, death rates and migration. Projections based on the mid-year estimates of population are produced by the Government Actuary's Department and published by OPCS in *OPCS Monitor PP2, Population Projections.*

Population projections have been produced since 1919 and between 1955 and 1979, national projections were produced every year. Following the Rayner Review, detailed projections are now made only every two years, that is, 1983-based, 1985-based, 1987-based etc.

These projections are usually published approximately a year after the mid-year estimate on which they are based. For example, the 1987-based population projections were published in the autumn of 1988. The published projections give data, by sex and age, up to 40 years ahead. The 1983-based projections, for example, give data up to the year 2023.

In 1989, a new series of interim projections was published for the first time, also in the OPCS Monitor PP2 series, in response to requests from users. These interim projections are based on the estimated population in the years when a full projection is not produced and the first set is based on the estimated population at the middle of the year 1988. Long-term assumptions remain the same but these interim projections take into account data about population changes which have become available since the last full projection was made.

Since 1965, OPCS has used the national projections as a base for producing sub-national projections and these are published in the OPCS Monitor PP3 series. Data is available for standard regions, London boroughs, metropolitan counties and districts, non-metropolitan counties, health regions and health districts. More detailed information covering other areas is available from OPCS on request.

In 1989, for the first time, OPCS produced extrapolated estimates for each local authority and health authority in England. These are short-term projections, for two years ahead, based on simple assumptions where the effects can be calculated relatively quickly. The first set of projections assumed that births, deaths and migration trends would remain unchanged for another two years. These

Table 3.3 OPCS annual statistical titles

Series DH	***Deaths*** (5 annual volumes)
Series FM	***Family Statistics*** (2 annual volumes)
Series MB	***Morbidity*** (3 annual volumes)
Series AB	***Abortion Statistics***
Series DR	***Demographic Review***
Series DS	***Decennial Supplement***
Series EL	***Electoral Statistics***
Series MN	***Internal Migration***
Series VS	***Vital Statistics***

extrapolated estimates were based on the mid-1988 population and provided projections for mid-1989 and mid-1990.

Other population statistics

Basic population statistics, plus articles and reviews on population issues, are published in the quarterly *Population Trends*. Up-to-date figures on births and deaths are produced weekly in the *Registrar General's Weekly Return for England and Wales*. The Registrar General in Scotland publishes the *Four Weekly Vital Statistics Return of the Registrar General, Scotland* along with quarterly figures. Quarterly data also comes from the Northern Ireland Registrar General. The Registrar General's offices also produce annual reports. *Key Population and Vital Statistics* provides figures for local authorities and health authorities in England and Wales.

Apart from the *OPCS Monitors* already mentioned relating to population estimates and projections, other individual titles cover abortions (AB), deaths by cause (DH2), infant and perinatal statistics (DH3), deaths from accidents and violence (DH4), electoral statistics (EL), infectious diseases (MB2) and social surveys (SS). These Monitors appear regularly, with provisional figures, and the codes in brackets refer to the code given to each monitor title.

OPCS Monitors giving provisional census data are published, when appropriate, and a separate monitor gives the provisional results of the *General Household Survey* (GHS) which is described in

Chapter 4. Various annual volumes of statistics cover specific demographic areas and the major series are listed in Table 3.3.

Non-official statistics: local government population data

Outside central government, the major sources of population data are local authorities. Local government population statistics are usually one of two varieties: either repackaged central government data or original data from a local authority survey. Many authorities publish annual population estimates of their area, and smaller local areas within their boundaries, based on the population estimates from central government. Every ten years when the population census data starts to appear, some authorities analyse the local results and publish census reports covering their locality or compile specific reports on particular wards and parishes within their area.

In other instances, authorities have established their own population surveys and are producing their own population projections although the number responsible for original data remains relatively small. The fact that most authorities still rely heavily on OPCS data is emphasized by a survey of county councils in 1990 (Coldicott, 1990). The survey looked at local authority attitudes to OPCS's mid-year estimates of population and asked councils whether they relied on OPCS data or produced their own statistics. Altogether 39 councils replied, representing an 85 per cent response rate, with 26 stating that they used OPCS estimates and 13 noting that they prepared their own estimates.

The problems associated with compiling OPCS estimates and projections have been described in previous sections of this chapter and, where local authorities are using OPCS data, many express reservations about the accuracy of the figures. The usual suggestion is that the population changes identified by OPCS are out of step with the local evidence of population change. In the above survey, three-quarters of those local authorities using OPCS data had some reservations about the statistics.

Inevitably, the arguments about population changes can often become more acute when figures for a local area are being produced separately by central government and a local authority. Differences often occur in the two sets of figures largely due to different methods of compilation and, in the case of projections, different assumptions underlying the projections. Sometimes these differences are small but, in other instances, they produce clearly conflicting results.

4 Socio-economic Data

Socio-economic statistics provide data on topics such as the economic position, living conditions, spending and ownership patterns, health, education and activities, attitudes and behaviour of the population. Public sector organizations, planning and monitoring services for specific population groups, have traditionally been major users of these statistics. The breakdown of mass markets and the increasing interest in market segmentation has also emphasized the importance of these statistics for many business users. Companies, particularly in the consumer goods and services sectors, are increasingly looking to target individual products at particular sectors of the population.

A general source of information on socio-economic topics is *Social Trends* published by central government. There are also three continuous official surveys, *General Household Survey*, *Family Expenditure Survey* and the *National Food Survey*. All these sources are described in the next section of this chapter but the major growth in socio-economic statistics has occurred in the non-official sector. In particular, there has been the development of geo-demographic services run by private companies and described later in this chapter.

Classification schemes

Many socio-economic statistics are based on particular classification schemes which categorize the population into certain types. Traditional classification schemes include classifications by occupation (see Chapter 7), income and social class. The income classification is used in the *National Food Survey*. Households are grouped into eight income groups – A1, A2, B, C, D, E1, E2, OAP – according to the income of the head of household.

The most widely used classification is the one covering social class, which breaks down the population into various categories, based on the occupation of the head of household:

- A Higher managerial, administrative, or professional
- B Intermediate managerial, administrative, or professional
- C1 Supervisory or clerical, and junior managerial, administrative, or professional
- C2 Skilled manual workers
- D Semi and unskilled manual workers
- E State pensioners or widows (no other earners), casual or lowest grade workers, or long-term unemployed

With the modern desire to segment markets, these traditional classifications are no longer always considered adequate with businesses looking for more refined and up-to-date categorizations of the population, based on their lifestyles and behaviour.

This has produced various new classification systems, such as Acorn, Pinpoint, Mosaic and Persona, described in the section on geo-demographics near the end of the chapter. These classifications provide a much more detailed breakdown than traditional social class definitions and include categories such as 'New Detached Houses, Young Families', 'Older Terraces, Lower Income Families' and 'Villages with Wealthy Older Communities'.

This apparent need to label people according to their lifestyles and habits has also produced a new breed of acronyms in the marketing and advertising world to classify different market segments. Most of these acronyms originate in the USA where, some years ago, the term WASP was coined to depict White Anglo-Saxon Protestants. The term 'yuppy' is now part of our everyday language but it first appeared as a marketing acronym in the mid 1980s. Its original marketing definition was young urban professional but, at some stage, this became young upwardly mobile professional and, in general use, it is often used as a derogatory term to describe rich and selfish young people.

After yuppy came various modifications including puppies (pregnant), muppies (middle-aged yuppies) and guppies (gay) and now

Table 4.1 Acronyms used to classify population groups

Yuppy	Young Upwardly Mobile Professional
Grumpies	Grim, Ruthless Upwardly Mobile Professionals
Swells	Single Women Earning Lots and Lots
Glams	Greys Leisured Affluent Married
Opals	Older People with Active Lifestyles
Dinkys	Dual Income No Kids Yet
Diwks	Dual Income with Kids
Dins	Dual Income, No Sex (too busy!)
Yuckee	Young Unemployed College Kid with an Economic Emergency
Sitcom*	Single Income, Two Children, Outrageous Mortgage

* Sitcom is not a generally recognised acronym but was sent by a reader as a suggestion to *The Economist*

the marketing world is awash with other acronyms including glams, opals and dinkies. Some of the major acronyms in use are given in Table 4.1 but new ones are emerging all the time.

The traditional classification schemes are still used as the basis for most official statistics and the newer schemes are usually found in the non-official sector.

Official statistics

To appreciate the range of social statistics produced by Central Government, a good starting point is *Social Trends* published annually by the CSO.

Social Trends

Social Trends was first published in 1968 and brings together statistics from many official sources plus a selection of non-official sources. It is arranged in 12 chapters corresponding closely to the administrative functions of government and the subjects covered by these chapters are listed in Table 4.2. Articles on selected social issues and social

Table 4.2 Subjects covered by *Social Trends*

Population
Households and Families
Education
Employment
Income and Wealth
Expenditure and Resources
Health and Personal Social Services
Housing
Transport and the Environment
Leisure
Participation (i.e., religion, charities etc.)
Law Enforcement

statistics are included in each issue. The key statistics from *Social Trends* are also published in another annual publication, *Key Data*, described as a student edition.

The publication concentrates on current policy issues and this is reflected in the nature and amount of information contained in individual sections. For example, the 1990 issue has an expanded section on the environment which is double the size of the sections in previous issues. *Social Trends* also tries to reflect the prevailing attitudes in society: in its early issues, figures on cigarette smoking appeared in the section on leisure but now these figures are included in the section on health.

Unlike most other official statistical publications, *Social Trends* uses various methods to present the statistics, including graphs, tables and charts, and each statistical section includes key data rather than a mass of statistics. These statistical sections are combined with brief simple commentaries on each subject area and the result is a publication which is attractive and relatively easy to use. This style of statistical presentation was unique when it first appeared in 1968 and it remains one of the few government statistical publications to combine commentary and data in this way.

Family Expenditure Survey (FES)

The Family Expenditure Survey (FES) primarily measures household spending on goods and services, that is, how much households spend and what they spend it on. It also provides additional information on household incomes and the characteristics of households.

The FES began in 1957 and its main purpose was to provide source data for reweighting the index of retail prices. Since 1962, information from it has been used for annually reweighting the retail price index and two pensioner indices but it also provides a considerable amount of useful economic and social data.

The CSO has overall responsibility for the FES but the collection of data is carried out by OPCS in Great Britain. Since 1967, a separate FES has been conducted in Northern Ireland by the Policy Planning and Research Unit of the Department of Finance and Personnel.

The FES is a continuous survey of a representative sample of private households in the UK and the sample is drawn from the Postcode Address File (PAF). Up to 1986, the sample was taken from the Electoral Registers but this source has particular limitations, notably its poor coverage of recent movers and aliens.

In 1989, a total sample of 12 805 addresses was selected in the UK: 11 605 in Great Britain and 1 200 in Northern Ireland. Approximately 14 per cent of the sample were ineligible addresses and some eligible addresses contained more than one household so the effective sample was equivalent to around 1 in every 2 000 households. In Great Britain, 73 per cent of the sample households co-operated in 1989 compared with 71 per cent in 1988 and 72 per cent in 1987. In Northern Ireland, the response rate was only 56 per cent. A third of the Northern Ireland sample is incorporated in the total FES results.

Fieldworkers visit co-operating households and carry out interviews with household members and ask them to maintain detailed expenditure records for 14 consecutive days. These records cover various products and services coded under approximately 250 headings. At the interview, household members are asked for details of all regularly recurring items of expenditure such as rates, rents and fuel and details of regular earnings. Additional information is obtained on the ownership of various consumer durables.

Each member of the household is paid £5 for their co-operation and interviews are spread evenly throughout the year ensuring that any seasonal expenditure changes are covered. The interview and the 14-day record produces information on the topics listed in Table 4.3. All expenditure and income values are converted to weekly equivalents then the data is processed and the results are published.

The major publication from the survey is an annual volume titled *Family Spending* (up to 1991 the volume title was *Family Expenditure*

Table 4.3 Information in the *Family Expenditure Survey*

Household characteristics:
Region and type of administrative area
Composition of household, including age and sex
Living accommodation – numbers of rooms/garage
Whether owned or rented
Rateable value and rate poundage*
Gas/electricity supply
Telephone installed
Television owned or rented
Washing machine/refrigerator
Central heating by type of fuel
Availability of motor vehicle (s)

Household expenditure:
Regular spending on rent, mortgage, rates*, HP, insurance
Expenditure on specific items during 14-day period

Household income and employment:
Employment status of individuals employed/self-employed/retired, absence through illness, holidays etc.
Occupation and industry of individuals
Earnings from occupations and self-employment earnings
Investment income
Social security benefits, including pensions
Occupational pensions, annuities
Imputed income from owner occupation

* included in the latest published FES although rates now abolished

Survey 199–), which is published in the year after the year in which the survey took place. The results of the 1989 survey were published in 1990. The annual volume has data on household characteristics plus expenditure data for specific categories of goods and services in total and by income, by household type, by household composition and by tenure. There are also income tables and tables covering household characteristics, expenditure and income by region.

Quarterly data from the FES is published in the statistical section of the monthly *Employment Gazette* (see Chapter 7 for further details) and preliminary results and key results from the FES are also published in regular articles in the *Employment Gazette*. As with most other government surveys, a large amount of unpublished data is available, on request, from the Department of Employment.

In both the expenditure and income sectors of the FES, there are one or two limitations which should be borne in mind when using the data. First, averages of household income in the FES are probably on the low side primarily because certain types of income, such as income from investments, occupational pensions and self-employment, are likely be underestimated. However, the main weakness on the income side is the underestimation of earnings from women in part-time employment.

On the expenditure side, reported expenditure on certain items, particularly alcohol and tobacco, are usually low compared to other sources of information on these products. For example, the estimated average expenditure of all households on beer is around two-thirds of what could be expected from figures in other statistical series produced by HM Customs and Excise. This low estimation is largely due to non-response from heavy drinkers and smokers.

Expenditure on items such as confectionery, soft drinks and ice cream is also low partly because most of these items form part of children's pocket money purchases and are often not reported separately by FES respondents. Pocket money is a category in its own right in the FES.

Expenditure on many household durables is likely to be underestimated by the FES since many of these items will not be purchased in the 14-day period. For the first time in the FES for 1989, expenditure estimates for certain items, notably floor coverings and furniture, have been based on information covering a three-month recall period in an attempt to improve the reliability of the expenditure estimates. This three-month recall period is likely to be extended to cover other suitable products in future surveys.

National Food Survey (NFS)

Specific information on the consumption and expenditure of food comes from the National Food Survey (NFS), a continuous survey carried out throughout the year. The survey, which began in 1940 and in its present form in 1952, also collects supplementary data on household characteristics.

It is based on a random sample of private households selected from

52 local authority districts and the survey itself is carried out by OPCS and the market research company, British Market Research Bureau (BMRB). OPCS selects the sample and BMRB carries out the fieldwork. The Ministry of Agriculture, Fisheries and Food (MAFF) is responsible for analysing and reporting the results.

As with the FES, the sample frame for the survey is based on the Postcode Address File (PAF). Households participate in the survey on a voluntary basis and there is no payment for co-operation. The sole respondent in the house is the person, male or female, 'principally responsible for domestic arrangements' and the NFS still refers to this person as the 'housewife'.

For the 1989 survey, a sample of 13 292 households was selected but the number of responding households was only 7 739 or 58 per cent of the selected sample. The relatively small percentage of responding households is due to a number of factors. Generally, responses are lower than in the FES and General Household Survey because, unlike these two surveys, no payment is involved and interviewers have less time to contact potential households. In 1989, with 2 004 cases, the households were visited but no contact with the housewife was made and in another 1 671 cases this person refused to give any information. In 11 237 households, the relevant person was contacted and 69 per cent of these provided information.

The relevant person is asked to keep a diary for seven days containing information on all the food entering the home each day that is intended for human consumption. Meals eaten outside the home and pet foods are excluded. Each item of food is described and details of the quantity and cost of the items are also included.

A few categories of food, such as chocolates, confectionery and alcoholic drinks, are excluded from the survey because they are likely to be purchased by individual family members, often without the knowledge of the so-called housewife. Soft drinks also fall into this category: since 1975, information about soft drinks bought for the household supply has been collected and the results are included in the annual report of the survey but the information is excluded from the main analyses because of the likelihood of under-recording.

In addition to the information for specific foods, the respondent also maintains notes on people present at each mealtime and the food served. The number and nature of meals obtained outside the home are also recorded. General data on the characteristics of the household are listed on a separate questionnaire.

The main results of the survey are published in an annual volume

Table 4.4 Main food groups covered by the NFS

Milk and cream
Cheese
Meat and meat products
Fish
Eggs
Fats and oils
Sugar and preserves
Fruit and vegetables
Bread, cereals and other cereal products
Beverages
Miscellaneous foods

titled *Household Food Consumption and Expenditure* while a MAFF press release describes the key results. The main section of the published report contains statistics and a brief analysis of the consumption and expenditure for the main food groups in aggregate and by household characteristics. Consumption and expenditure is also analysed by region, income group and household composition.

The food groups covered by the survey are listed in Table 4.4. Data also cover the number of meals eaten outside the home and the expenditure on these meals. Other sections look at the nutritional value of the household diet and the way in which consumption patterns for particular foods are affected by changes in income, prices and other factors.

General Household Survey (GHS)

The GHS is the youngest of the three continuous socio-economic surveys carried out by central government. It began in 1971 with the aim of obtaining a range of information on households, social groups and social indicators in Great Britain. It is carried out by OPCS although various departments are actually involved in the development of the topics to be covered. A similar survey, the Continuous Household Survey, was established in 1983 for Northern Ireland and this is conducted by the Policy Planning and Research Unit of the Department of Finance and Personnel.

Questions on major topic areas such as housing, migration,

Table 4.5 GHS – key topics covered continuously

Housing – including tenure, amenities, durables, housing type and age
Internal Migration
Employment – including job description, unemployment
Education – including type of educational establishment, leaving age, qualifications
Health – including chronic and acute sickness, doctor consultations, out-patient attendances, in-patient stays, use of selected health and personal social services
Household and Family Information – including compositions and demographic characteristics, socio-economic group, income, number of children, marital history, ethnic group

employment, education, health and family characteristics have been included continuously since the survey began while other topics appear for only a few years or are included only occasionally. For example, in 1988 questions on young people's drinking habits were asked for the first time and in 1987 and 1988, share ownership questions appeared for the first time. Tables 4.5 and 4.6 show both sets of topics.

The survey is based on a sample of the resident population in private households in Great Britain. The sample is now 12 400 having been reduced from 14 564 in 1982 following a Rayner Committee recommendation. In the 1988 survey, interviews were carried out with 10 242 responding households comprising 19 716 people.

Information for the GHS is collected throughout the year through personal interviews with all members of a household over 16 years of age. Parents are also asked certain questions about the health and education of children under 16. The GHS asks a variety of questions but respondents are not obliged to, or may not be able to, answer every single question.

Unlike other continuous surveys, partial responses are usually included in the GHS results and this means that response rates are usually higher than these other surveys. The response rate is split into three categories: in 1988, the minimum response rate, including

Table 4.6 GHS – topics included occasionally 1971–1988

Absence from Work (1971–84)
Activities on School Premises (1984)
Dental Health (1983, 1985, 1987)
Difficulties with Eyesight (1977–79, 1981–82, 1987)
Difficulties with Hearing (1977–79, 1981)
Drinking Habits (1978, 1980, 1982, 1984, 1986, 1988)
Driving Licences (1980)
Elderly Persons (1980, 1985)
Entertainments, Libraries, Forests (1987)
Household Burglary (1972–73, 1979–80, 1985–86)
Job Mobility (1971–87)
Leisure (1973, 1977, 1980, 1983, 1986)
Loans Raised on the Security of the Home (1980–82)
Occupational Pension Schemes (1987–88)
Share Ownership (1987–88)
Sitting Tenants (1980–87)
Smoking Habits (1972–76, 1978, 1980, 1982, 1984, 1986, 1988)
Type of Fuel Used by Private Households (1978–81, 1983, 1985)
Voluntary Work (1981, 1987)

only those people who answered all the questions, was 74 per cent; the maximum response rate, which accepts all partial responses in the results, was 87 per cent; the middle response rate, which includes some of the partial answers, and is used as the performance indicator for the survey was 85 per cent.

An OPCS Monitor gives preliminary results from the latest GHS before the detailed report is published. For example, preliminary results from the 1989 GHS were published in an OPCS Monitor in October 1989 but the detailed published results usually appear some months later in the annual *General Household Survey*. The 1988 GHS report was not published until 1990.

Separate reports are also published on selected special topics. A supplementary report titled *Drinking* was published from the 1986 GHS and *Participation in Sport* and *Voluntary Work* were supplementary titles from the 1987 GHS. More detailed unpublished data can be supplied by the Social Survey Division of OPCS.

Non-official statistics

General sources

British Social Attitudes Series
Since 1983, a company called Social and Community Planning Research (SCPR) has been undertaking an annual survey of people's attitudes to a range of social, political, economic and moral issues. The types of topics covered by the survey include social welfare, the family, environment, self-employment and the enterprise culture, health, individualism and the moral climate. The main results of the survey appear annually in *British Social Attitudes: the 199– Report* published by Gower. In 1992, SCPR began producing an annual cumulative sourcebook of key findings.

The aim of the survey is to discover people's underlying attitudes, so that long-term trends in the nation's values can be monitored. It does not attempt to find out what people's opinions are on topical issues or personalities and this area is left to the opinion pollsters described in a later section.

The main source of data for this series is an annual interview survey, plus a self-completion questionnaire, with a sample of 3 000 people aged over 18 in Great Britain. In 1990, the published volume included results from Northern Ireland for the first time based on replies from 900 respondents.

In the early annual surveys, only 1 800 people were interviewed but in recent years, the number has increased to 3 000. This allows the survey to ask some questions of a random half of the sample and other questions of the remaining half. Some topics such as politics and political culture, social policy, welfare, public spending, moral and family issues are covered on a regular basis while other topics appear less frequently. For example, in the 1990 survey, questions on attitudes to trade unions were asked for the first time.

The survey is funded by the Sainsbury Family Charitable Trust with supplementary funds from a number of government departments, quasi-governmental bodies and other foundations and companies.

There are also links with other countries through the International Social Survey Programme which SCPR co-founded in 1985. Each year, a set of identical questions on a rotating group of topics is asked in 14 countries and the comparative results are placed in the Data

Archive at the University of Cologne in Germany where they are publicly available. Apart from the UK, the countries currently collaborating in the scheme are Australia, Austria, Hungary, Ireland, Israel, Italy, Netherlands, Norway, USA and West Germany.

CIPFA Statistics

CIPFA is the Chartered Institute of Public Finance and Accountancy and its statistical information service publishes a series of titles on local government and public sector services and finances. Each service area, such as environmental health, housing, education and police, has its own annual publication. These publications contain financial, and related data such as employment figures, covering the administration and operation of the various services in individual local authority areas in England and Wales.

As well as financial data, most of the titles contain additional data on the nature, extent and use of services and facilities in specific local areas. For example, the publication *Leisure and Recreation Statistics* has figures on the number of golf courses, leisure centres, theatres and allotments in specific local authority areas.

CIPFA publishes two general annual compilations of statistics, *Local Government Comparative Statistics* with general data on specific local authorities, and *Local Government Trends* with commentary and statistics on individual services but no detailed local authority breakdown. Table 4.7 has details of CIPFA's specific titles.

Opinion polls

Public opinion polls try to find out people's attitudes and opinions on topical issues and personalities at a particular moment in time. Key polling organizations in the UK include Audience Selection, Social Surveys (Gallup Poll) Ltd, Harris, Marplan, MORI, NOP and ICM and, in most people's minds, they are associated with opinion polls on political issues.

Certainly, the number of political polls has increased in recent years – Table 4.8 shows that 63 national polls were carried out during the 1987 general election campaign compared to only 26 in 1979 – but political opinion polling is usually only a small part of the work of a polling organization.

Gallup, for example, states that political polls account for only 5 per cent of its total turnover. Polls on other issues are carried out for a range of organizations including private companies, academic institutions and public authorities and the following are some examples.

Table 4.7 Subjects covered by regular CIPFA statistics

Administration of Justice
Airports
Archives
Capital Expenditure and Debt Financing
Cemeteries
Crematoria
Community Charges
Direct Labour Organizations
Education
Environmental Health
Finance and General
Fire
Homelessness
Housing Rents
Housing Revenue Account
Leisure and Recreation
Leisure Charges
Leisure Usage
Personal Social Services
Planning and Development
Police
Probation
Public Libraries
Rating Review (Scotland)
Smallholdings
Trading Standards
Waste Collection
Waste Disposal

In 1991, Nationwide Building Society commissioned Audience Selection to carry out a telephone survey of over 1 500 people to discover their awareness of and knowledge about TESSAs.

In 1988 and 1989, the Department of the Environment commissioned NOP to survey people's attitudes to the environment. In 1987, NOP carried out a survey of share ownership for the Treasury.

In 1989, the paints company Crown Berger commissioned Gallup to survey people's opinions on a range of topics including quality of life,

Table 4.8 National opinion polls in election campaigns

Year	Number
1970	25
1974 Feb	25
1974 Oct	27
1979	26
1983	49
1987	63

fashion in the home, leisure, conservation and the shopping experience.

Gallup carries out a regular survey of the cookware market for the company, Du Pont and a weekly survey of over 700 record shops to compile music charts.

Traditionally, information for polls has been collected through face-to-face interviews with a random sample of people, usually at selected geographical points around the country. Samples can vary in size but, in general, sample sizes have been getting bigger. In 1979, the average national political poll size was 1 323 but, by 1987, this average had risen to 1 550.

The 1980s have also seen the growth of telephone interviewing in opinion poll surveys. In the early 1980s, telephone interviews were only used in certain circumstances because not everyone was on the telephone and those that were skewed to the young and affluent. Now, telephone ownership is much more widespread and telephone polling has increased.

Most of the polling organizations also offer a range of other services including attitude surveys, omnibus surveys, tracking surveys, ad hoc research and retail audits. These types of surveys are discussed in more detail in Chapter 8.

Omnibus surveys are a relatively cheap source of socio-economic data. These involve interviews with a sample of people on a regular basis, perhaps weekly or monthly. Subscribers to the survey can have their own questions included in it and the costs of the survey are distributed over all participating subscribers. Survey results are usually available within a few days of the survey taking place and, in addition to the specific questions asked, the social and demographic characteristics of the respondents can be analysed and provided as results.

Gallup, for example, has a weekly omnibus survey interviewing a national sample of 2 000 adults aged 16 and over (1 000 men and 1 000 women). The basic price per question to the subscriber for 1 000 interviews is £250 and the report of the survey is normally available within four days of the completion of the survey.

Generally available publications provide summary data from the main political, social and economic polls carried out by Gallup, MORI and NOP. The *Gallup Political and Economic Index* is published by Dod's Publishing and Research Ltd, the *Political, Social and Economic Review* is published by NOP and *British Public Opinion* is produced ten times a year by MORI.

Geo-demographic services

Traditionally, social classifications have been based on conventional socio-economic criteria, such as income or social class. Many of the official publications still use these classifications with the most common being the AB, C1, C2, DE social class breakdown. In the late 1970s and 1980s, the traditional notion of social class had less appeal and, with the emphasis on market segmentation and niche marketing, marketers looked for new ways to describe people and more precise ways to target specific consumer groups and types.

Geo-demographic services can provide detailed demographic statistics for very localized areas based on classifications of small areas according to the characteristics of their inhabitants. Geo-demographics makes two assumptions: two people living in the same neighbourhood are more likely to have similar characteristics than two people chosen at random; neighbourhoods can be categorized in terms of the population which they contain and two neighbourhoods can be placed in the same category even though they may be at different ends of the country.

There are four main geo-demographic services in the UK, all using their own classifications of local neighbourhoods, but all based on the assumptions that people with similar lifestyles and buying habits live in the same type of neighbourhood. Two examples of the classifications used are given in Tables 4.9 and 4.10.

The services are based on an analysis of detailed population census data plus additional data from various sources including credit records, electoral rolls and market research surveys.

Table 4.9 Pinpoint identified neighbourhoods: classification summary labels

12 LEVEL PiN TYPES		25 LEVEL PiN TYPES		60 LEVEL PiN TYPES	
A RURAL	(5.14)	a Farmers & Agricultural Workers	(1.22)	1 highest proportion of agricultural workers	(0.06)
				2 managerial with families	(0.01)*
				3 small farms and smallholdings	(0.08)
				4 with elderly	(0.20)
				5 with other occupations	(0.71)
				6 lacking amenities	(0.16)
		b Rural Villages	(3.92)	7 commuter belt	(1.09)
				8 villagers	(2.83)
B ARMED FORCES	(0.30)	c Armed Forces	(0.30)	9 with growing children	(0.14)
				10 with large houses	(0.01)*
				11 many young children	(0.16)
				12 many aged 16–24	(0.01)
C UPWARDLY MOBILE YOUNG FAMILIES	(14.12)	d Country Towns	(0.79)	13 with armed forces	(0.49)
				14 many professionals	(0.30)
		e Families with Growing Children	(8.96)	15 in established industrial areas	(7.07)
				16 well off	(1.89)
		f Young Couples and Small Children	(4.47)	17 many small children	(2.89)
				18 many working women	(1.39)
D AFFLUENT HOUSEHOLDS	(10.13)	g Wealthy	(7.37)	19 wealthy	(7.34)
		h Very Wealthy	(2.69)	20 exclusive residential areas	(0.28)
				21 most affluent residential areas	(2.40)
E OLDER PEOPLE IN SMALL HOUSES	(11.50)	i Council Flats with Pensioners	(2.19)	22 council flats with pensioners	(2.19)
		J Comfortable Retirement Areas	(2.31)	23 comfortable retirement areas	(2.31)
		k Council Housing with Elderly	(7.01)	24 council housing with elderly	(7.01)
F SUBURBAN MIDDLE AGED OR OLDER	(17.04)	l Owner Occupied with Elderly	(9.15)	25 owner occupied with elderly	(9.15)
		m Large Houses, Some Divided into Flats	(2.59)	26 large houses, some divided into flats	(2.59)
		n Suburban Commuters	(5.29)	27 suburban commuters	(5.29)

Table 4.9 concluded

G	WORKING PEOPLE WITH FAMILIES	(10.26)	o	Working People with Families	(10.26)	28 working people with families	(10.26)
H	POOR URBAN AREAS	(6.14)	p	Unmodernized Private Dwellings	(5.87)	29 larger dwellings	(4.76)
						30 smaller dwellings	(1.11)
			q	Deprived Areas	(0.27)	31 least deprived	(0.22)
						32 small flats with young people	(0.04)
						33 lacking bath and wc	(0.01)
						34 agricultural workers	(0.01)*
						35 most overcrowded, many Asians	(0.01)*
						36 with owner occupied housing	(0.01)*
I	LOW STATUS AREAS WITH FLATS	(5.82)	r	Poor Small Dwellings	(2.61)	37 poorest young people	(0.39)
						38 city council flats	(0.24)
						39 city outskirts and large towns	(1.98)
			s	Small Urban Flats	(3.21)	40 many young adults and immigrants	(1.05)
						41 smallest flats	(0.85)
						42 many in Social class I	(0.01)*
						43 many young single people	(0.07)
						44 in city areas with fewest children	(1.22)
J	INNER CITY BEDSITS	(1.12)	t	Inner City Bedsits	(1.12)	45 few middle aged	(0.13)
						46 many young adults and immigrants	(0.18)
						47 better areas with some large houses	(0.27)
						48 mixed ages and occupations	(0.41)
						49 office workers	(0.12)
						50 highest concentrations	(0.01)*
						51 crowded	(0.02)
K	POOR MULTI-ETHNIC AREAS	(2.19)	u	Poor Multi-ethnic Areas	(2.19)	52 medium-sized housing	(0.75)
						53 many born Africa/Caribbean	(1.08)
						54 many born India, Bangladesh, Pakistan	(0.01)*
						55 large young families	(0.35)
L	CROWDED COUNCIL NEIGHBOURHOODS	(16.27)	v	Overcrowded Estates with Young Children	(3.34)	56 with immigrants	(1.84)
						57 large young families	(1.50)
			w	Crowded Estates	(2.57)	58 crowded estates	(2.57)
			x	Poor Estates	(6.90)	59 poor estates	(6.90)
			y	With Growing Up Children	(3.46)	60 with growing up children	(3.46)

Figures in brackets show the size of each PiN type as a percentage of all United Kingdom households (excluding Northern Ireland).
N.B. * are those PiN types with percentages less than 0.01%

Source: Pinpoint Analysis Ltd.

Table 4.10 Descriptions of the 58 Mosaic postcode types

M1	High status retirement areas with many single persons
M2	High status retirement areas, married owner occupiers
M3	High status retirement areas with rented flats for elderly
M4	Boarding houses and lodgings, many in retirement areas
M5	Inter-war O/O housing, commercial and managerial cadres
M6	Elite prof/educational suburbs, mostly inner metropolitan
M7	High status family enclaves in inner city areas
M8	Highest income and status areas, mostly outer metropolitan
M9	Inter-war semis, white collar commuters to urban office jobs
M10	Inter-war semis, owner occupied by well paid manual workers
M11	Areas of mixed tenure, many old people
M12	Lower income enclaves in high income suburbs
M13	Older suburbs, young families in Gov't and service emp't
M14	Older terraces, owner occupied by craft manual workers
M15	Lower income older terraced housing
M16	Overcrowded older houses, often in areas of housing shortage
M17	Older terraces, young families in very crowded conditions
M18	Tenements, caravans & other rented temporary accommodation
M19	Town centres and flats above shops
M30	Post-1981 extensions to high stress inner city areas
M31	High unemployment estates with worst financial problems
M32	Council estates with the highest levels of unemployment
M33	Council estates, often Scottish flats, with worst crowding
M34	Better council estates but with financial problems
M35	Low-rise council housing, low incomes & serious deprivation
M36	Areas with some public housing for the elderly
M37	Council estates, mostly Scottish, middle income small houses
M38	Council estates in factory towns with settled older workers
M39	Quality 30s and 50s overspill estates, now with old people
M40	Best quality council housing in areas of low unemployment
M41	New greenfield council estates with many young children
M42	Post 1981 council housing, higher incomes
M43	Post 1981 council housing, few families
M44	Post 1981 council housing with stable families
M45	Military accommodation
M46	Post 1981 housing in areas of highest income and status
M47	Highest income and status area, newish family housing
M48	Post war private estates with children of school age

Table 4.10 concluded

M20 Rented non family inner city areas with financial problems	M49 Newly built private estates, high income young families
M21 Low status inner suburbs with subdivided older housing	M50 Newly built private estates, factory workers, young families
M22 Older housing where owner occupiers often share with tenants	M51 Post 1981 extensions to private estates
M23 Purpose built private flats, single people in service jobs	M52 Post 1981 housing in established older suburbs
M24 Divided houses with mobile single people and few children	M53 New commuter estates in rural areas
M25 Smart inner city flats, company lets, very few children	M54 Villages with some non agricultural employment
M26 Post 1981 housing in non family urban and city centres	M55 Pretty rural villages with wealthy long distance commuters
M27 Post 1981 housing replacing older terraces	M56 Agricultural villages
M28 Newly built council housing, mostly high density inner city	M57 Hamlets and scattered farms
M29 Newly built inner city estates with non family populations	M58 Unclassified

Source: CCN Marketing Ltd.

Aggregate information on specific local areas can be supplied plus individual names and addresses for mailing lists. The services are used in areas such as store location exercises, direct mail campaigns and the monitoring of the use of outlets such as retail stores and leisure facilities. A typical subscription to one of these services would start at a few thousand pounds.

The four main classification systems are:

Acorn. Acorn stands for 'A Classification of Residential Neighbourhoods' and was the first system developed in the UK by the company, CACI, in 1979. The system has 38 neighbourhood types and every address in the UK is allocated to one of these types.

Pinpoint. Pinpoint Analysis Ltd was founded in 1983 and the PIN system (Pinpoint Identified Neighbourhoods) has 60 classified neighbourhoods. Details of these are shown in Table 4.9.

Mosaic. Mosaic is a classification comprising 58 neighbourhood types and run by CCN Marketing, established in the UK in 1980. The classification is shown in Table 4.10.

Superprofile. A classification of 150 neighbourhood types developed by the company, CDMS.

The range of services available from these organizations is considerable and expanding, including specific services for certain sectors such as retailing and financial services, and services supplying detailed local market research data through links with companies such as Nielsen.

On-line services are being produced by some of the services. GB-SITE, for example, is an on-line service produced by CACI containing socio-demographic data from recent population censuses supplemented with CACI forecasts and information from retail and media surveys.

The service has been produced as a companion database to the US SUPERSITE service and data is available for specific local areas, such as wards, parishes, local authorities and census enumeration districts. The above data can be linked with the ACORN data and the system is available via computer bureaux, DRI and WEFA (see Appendix 1 for details). Payment of a fixed fee gives unlimited use but charges can also be made per report.

The above systems are based on demographics and inclusion in a particular neighbourhood type points to the way in which a particular household or neighbourhood group of households is likely to behave.

Table 4.11 Persona behavioural types

Young Affluentials
Golf Clubs and Volvos
Bon Viveurs
Tradition and Charity
Achievers
Trinkets and Treasures
New Techers
Safe and Sensible
Health and Humanities
Craftsmen and Homemakers
Cultural Travellers
Carry on Camping
Wildlife Trustees
Field and Stream
Crisps and Videos
Fads and Fashions
Home and Garden
Pubs, Pools and Bingo
Survivors
Retired Villagers

The latest segmentation systems are refining the classification process by measuring the actual behaviour patterns of consumers.

One such system is Persona and this is based on a regular survey of over four million households. The survey, known as the National Shoppers' Survey (NSS), comprises a questionnaire sent by direct mail to consumers. Respondents who reply to the questionnaire receive, in return, promotional offers of interest to them. Survey questions cover areas such as products and brands bought, type of home owned or rented, occupations, cars owned, personal and family interests and leisure pursuits, holidays, community activities, home improvement activities and financial services used.

Using NSS data, Persona has created a classification of 20 different household types referred to as 'behavioural types', based on how they spend their working and leisure time and how they spend their money. A list of the nicknames used to describe these behavioural types is given in Table 4.11.

Miscellaneous sources

Daily Life in the 1980s

Every few years, the BBC carries out a detailed survey covering 15 000 people which looks at their media and leisure activities. Survey participants are asked to keep a diary of what they do in 15-minute segments throughout the day. Every activity, whether work or leisure related, is included.

The detailed results of this survey are published in various volumes with the general title of *Daily Life in the 19—s*. The latest survey took place in the middle of the 1980s and was published in 1989. More detailed results and analyses are available on request and an on-line version is available from Telmar Communications (see Appendix 1 for details).

Town Focus

This is an on-line service offered by the company Property Intelligence plc. The service provides individual town reports giving demographic, socio-economic and property data for over 600 locations throughout the UK. It covers all towns with populations over 20 000.

For each town, there is demographic data, including population projections, population profiles based on the Superprofile classification, communications data, information on rents and prices, planning data and contacts. The data is collected from various sources including the population census, Department of Employment, local authorities, academic research, CDMS, Nationwide Building Society and the property press.

Town Focus Plus is the off-line version with the same data available on floppy discs with additional software with which users can manipulate the data to select, rank and compare towns according to criteria they specify.

Demographic Profiles

The Unit for Retail Planning Information (URPI) offers a range of services relating to retailing and demographic trends. *Demographic Profiles* is a specific service providing profiles of the population in geographically defined areas such as towns, cities, local authority areas, and regions. Different levels of the service are available providing different degrees of detail. The information can be supplied in hard copy format or on disc and the database is continually updated.

Henley Centre

As well as its economic forecasts and industry surveys, the Centre carries out a regular Time Use Survey, in association with Millward Brown, the market research company. At the end of every calendar quarter, a sample of people are asked about their activity patterns over the previous three months. Summary results are published in the quarterly *Leisure Futures* with more detailed information available on request. Town and City Focus is a new consultancy service from Henley offering socio-economic data on Britain's major centres of population.

Other sources of socio-economic data include market research surveys, audience and readership surveys and marketing manuals from TV and radio companies. All these are described in more detail in Chapter 8.

5 Economic and Financial Data

Macro-economic and financial statistics are the most visible of all the statistical series and their publication can have a major impact on government policy, business expectations and the financial markets. Most of these are published by central government but other important publishers include the Bank of England and the Stock Exchange, associations in the financial sector, individual banks, stockbrokers and financial analysts, economic research and forecasting organizations, chambers of commerce and employers federations.

Statistics on areas such as retail prices, GDP and the balance of payments, are regularly quoted on radio and TV news and in the national press while the figures are debated and digested by politicians, financial analysts, business people, trade unionists, academics and the general public.

In the long term, economic statistics provide a continuous picture of the economic development and well being of a country. In the short term, a bad set of statistics can take billions off the value of shares, and vice versa, and the impact a particular statistical series can have is emphasized by the amount of time spent by commentators and analysts in trying to predict what the next set of statistics will show. If the actual figures live up to expectations, then the markets are likely to remain stable but if the published figures confound expectations, the markets are likely to react.

Businesses can change investment, output or employment

decisions in the light of a set of balance of payment or price figures while trade unions base their pay negotiations around the retail price index. Most importantly of all, central government base their decisions, and monitor and justify the decisions they take, on the various economic statistics for which they are responsible.

Official statistics

As economic and financial statistics are at the centre of the government's need for data, the accuracy and integrity of these statistics are vital. The CSO is responsible for most of the statistics and is an independent department responsible to the Chancellor of the Exchequer.

To prevent the political party in power manipulating the timing of the release of a particular set of statistics, the publication dates of the various economic statistics are laid down in advance. The release of bad figures cannot be postponed and good figures cannot be brought forward to suit a particular political end. Any attempt to manipulate the data by changing the definitions used and the way the statistics are collected is likely to be debated in parliament and in the wider public domain.

This, of course, does not stop changes but it opens up government statistical activity to rigorous public scrutiny. The most obvious example is the various changes that were made to the way in which unemployment statistics were collected between 1979 and 1990. These changes were accompanied by widespread debate with suggestions of political manipulation of the figures to attempt to make the unemployment numbers look smaller than they were. Defenders of the changes claimed that most of these were technically necessary and brought the series in line with other European countries.

Problem areas

In most cases, the integrity of official economic statistics remains intact but the accuracy of some of the series has been pushed to the limit with the growing complexity of the economy, the need for ever more up-to-date information and the reduction in resources devoted to statistical activities in the 1980s.

Many of the national economic and financial statistics are put together using data from various other statistical surveys. The Family

Expenditure Survey, for example, is used as the basis for calculating the retail price index, and monthly import and export figures are used to calculate parts of the balance of payments data. All the individual series used have their own particular problems and limitations, discussed in more detail in the relevant chapters of this book, and these weaknesses are likely to affect the eventual economic and financial series produced.

Changes in the economic mix, particularly changes in the boundaries between the public and private sectors coupled with the deregulation of economic activity, a hallmark of the Thatcher government in the 1980s, have made the collection of meaningful statistics more difficult. One example was the abolition of exchange controls which made it difficult to measure cross-border capital movements.

As more areas of economic activity are taken out of the public sector, the problems of measuring these areas become more acute. Deregulation has also been accompanied by the removal of the form-filling burden for many companies: smaller companies, plus those based in areas such as Enterprise Zones, are no longer required to complete statistical returns. C. Johnson states 'freedom of a kind has been obtained at the cost of statistical accuracy. At the limit, an economy free from any taint of interference by official statisticians might achieve a record rate of growth without ever being able to find out that it had done so' (Johnson, 1988).

The growing influence of multi-national companies and the rapid and complex changes in areas such as financial services have also created truly international sectors which are difficult to measure in isolation in the UK. As the economy becomes more complex and diverse, a more rigorous collection and analysis of statistical data is required but, in the UK, the response was to cut back the numbers employed in the Government Statistical Service.

To satisfy the demand for more up-to-date information, most of the major economic indicators are initially published in press releases. These are the figures usually quoted in the media and the ones which the markets react to yet they are often provisional figures which are later revised when they appear in the traditional statistical publications.

In other words, decisions are made based on figures which are at best misleading. The figures for trade in 'invisibles', for example, which form part of the balance of payments series are regularly revised, sometimes years after the original figures have appeared. The most notable case of misleading statistics in recent years concerned GDP statistics which, at the time of the 1988 Budget, failed to register the strength of domestic demand. The GDP figures misled the then Chancellor, Nigel Lawson, into presenting a tax-cutting budget which fuelled consumer spending and overheated the economy.

Various official economic series have been criticized in recent years and more detailed information on the statistics, and their limitations, are given in *Measuring the Economy: a guide to understanding official statistics* (Johnson, 1988). One or two key economic statistics receiving particular criticism have been the following:

Gross Domestic Product (GDP) statistics

There are three measures of GDP. GDP(O), or GDP output, measures the total output of goods and services in terms of valued-added. GDP(I), or GDP income, measures the total income derived from the produced output; and GDP(E), or GDP expenditure, measures expenditure on total output.

In theory, these measures are the same but, in practice, they differ because they are estimated by different statistical methods. In the 1980s, the divergences in the figures produced by these three measures widened 'to unacceptable levels' according to an article in the *Treasury Bulletin* (Hibberd, 1990, p. 2). At one stage, GDP(E) lagged 5.5 per cent below the measures for output and income, giving a distorted picture of the strength of the economy.

Estimates of some of the components of the GDP figures have been shown to be relatively inaccurate particularly those relating to company profits, a component of the income measure of GDP, capital expenditure, a component of the expenditure measure and stock-building, used in all three measures of GDP.

Retail Price Index (RPI)

The RPI measures the rate of change of consumer prices and is based on the prices of 600 different items sold in 180 areas in different regions and in different types of outlets. Each item is given a weight, which is the percentage of consumer expenditure represented by that item, according to the Family Expenditure Survey (FES). This immediately makes the RPI out-of-date because it is based on the expenditure patterns recorded in the FES approximately 18 months previously.

In 1986, The Retail Price Index Advisory Committee (RPIAC) stated that the monthly collection of price quotations for the RPI was unsystematic and that the number of quotations fell short of the maximum specified. It also called for the inclusion of additional items which represented significant items of consumer expenditure, according to the FES. For example, payments made in the UK for foreign holidays, fees for education, health, trade unions and professional bodies and certain financial services such as bank charges and insurance payments.

Housing costs, measured by mortgage interest costs, are included in the RPI although a number of other European countries exclude them from their price index. The problem is that changes in housing costs can be volatile, as in the mid- and late 1980s, and these can have a dramatic effect on the RPI. One argument states that home ownership is an investment, and certain measures of housing costs should not be included in the RPI. In reality, most people treat housing costs as part of the general cost of living. In order to reduce the fluctuations in the RPI caused by housing cost changes, the RPIAC recommended various changes to the way this item was calculated.

General details of the items covered by the RPI are given in Table 5.1.

Balance of payments

The balance of payments figures are based on estimates of the imports and exports of goods and services. Estimating the trade in goods (visibles) is relatively straightforward, although there are problems in the short term and these are described in more detail in Chapter 6. It means that the monthly and quarterly figures are subsequently revised at a later date but usually only by a small amount.

The real problems are associated with the estimates of 'invisible' trade, covering services, interest, profits and dividends and transfers. The nature of trade in invisibles means that collecting data is difficult. It is collected in a variety of ways and most of it on a quarterly basis. The monthly figures are therefore rough estimates which will be revised when the quarterly figures appear. Even the quarterly figures

Table 5.1 Structure of the Retail Prices Index in 1991

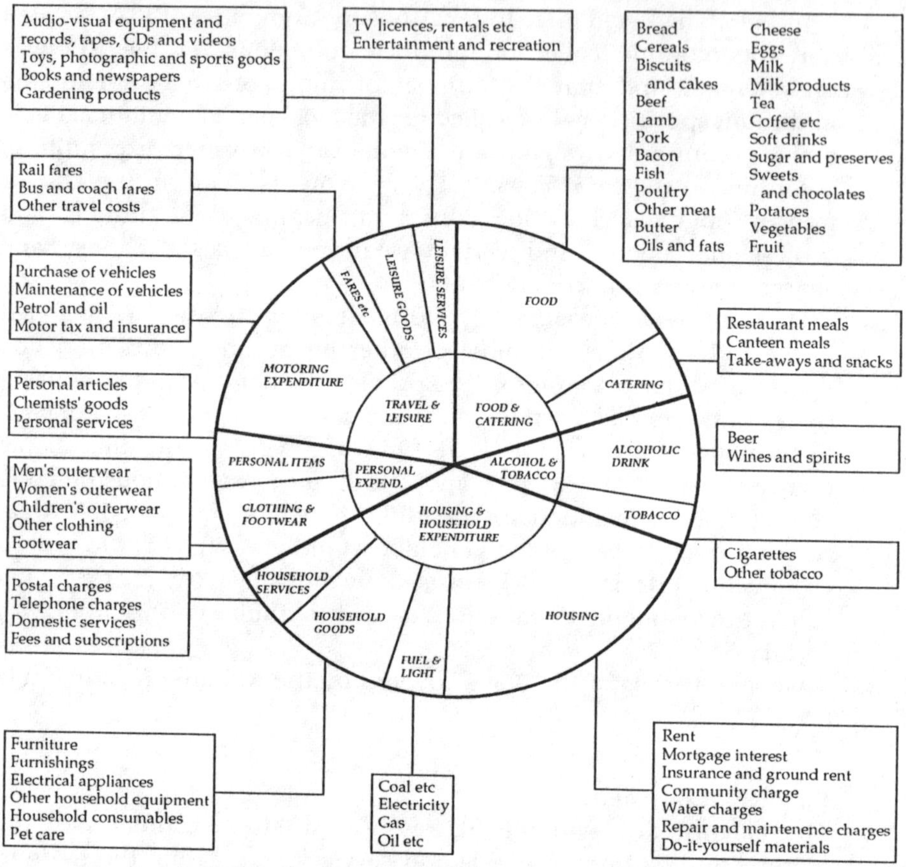

Source: Central Statistical Office

are likely to be incomplete, because of the difficulties of collection, and these will probably be revised on a number of occasions.

Changes and improvements

The above are just some of the problems associated with economic statistics and general disquiet over the accuracy of economic statistics led to a number of changes in the late 1980s.

An efficiency scrutiny examined inter-departmental arrangements for the production of economic statistics and made various recommendations in its final report (HMSO, 1989). One recommendation suggested a greater role for the CSO and, in 1989, the CSO was enlarged becoming a new government department responsible to the Chancellor of the Exchequer.

This change was designed to bring about a significant improvement in the quality of government economic statistics. The CSO took a greater direct responsibility for the compilation of the national accounts and for the associated collection of data from businesses. The director of the CSO stated that 'the main reason for the change is to bring under one management more of the work underlying the compilation of macro-economic statistics. This should make it possible to decide priorities and tackle problems in a more effective and co-ordinated way' (Central Statistical Office, 1989).

Concern had also been expressed by the Treasury and Civil Service Select Committee about the quality of the national accounts statistics, and in May 1990, the Chancellor announced a series of further measures to improve economic statistics (*Economic Trends*, 1991). Primarily, these measures were aimed at improving the statistics in three key areas: services, the company sector and the balance of payments. A further review of balance of payments statistics was initiated in 1990 to identify further improvements aimed at reducing the scale and frequency of revisions and the size of the balancing items.

A report from the Retail Price Index Advisory Committee (RPIAC) in 1986 called for changes in the way in which the Retail Price Index is collected and many of these changes have been implemented. Following the Chancellor's announcement, estimates of the components of GDP described earlier, that is company profits, capital expenditure and stockbuilding, are now collected through statutory inquiries rather than voluntary inquiries as before because 'only a statutory inquiry can produce estimates of acceptable quality'. A new set of statutory Quarterly Turnover Inquiries (QTI) covering selected parts of the service trades was also introduced in 1991 to help to improve the quarterly estimates of GDP(O).

In the final years of the 1980s, the national accounts estimates for the industrial and commercial company sector included a large balancing item of unidentified flows, largely due to the lack of information on the financial transactions of these companies. In 1991, the CSO introduced a statutory annual survey covering the financial assets and liabilities of approximately 700 large company groups with the aim of improving the national accounts estimates for the industrial and commercial company sector.

Improvements in official economic statistics are likely to continue in the early part of the 1990s, helped by the decision in 1990 to give the CSO an extra 100 staff. For the first time, some of the Rayner cuts are being reversed in recognition of the need for reliable economic statistics.

The key sources

Press releases

Virtually all of the releases covering economic and financial statistics are published by CSO and these are available through an annual subscription, either to the complete set or to releases covering specific indicators. Labour market press releases are published by the Department of Employment and described in Chapter 7. Money and banking releases come from the Bank of England (see later section of this chapter). The releases usually only show short-term trends and most contain basic statistics and a brief commentary.

Major economic indicators not covered by press releases are interest rates and exchange rates which are published daily in the press and in other sources such as *Financial Statistics* and *Bank of England Quarterly Bulletin*.

A list of the regular press releases published by CSO is given in Table 5.2, followed by brief comments on the major titles.

The retail price index, in its present form, began in 1962, although records of consumer prices were established long before that. The predecessor of the RPI was the national cost of living index established in 1914. The monthly press release is usually published on the second or third Friday after the month covered by the statistics. The index always refers to a Tuesday near the middle of each month although, in practice, it can often take longer than a day to collect all the local prices so some prices are collected on the Monday or Wednesday. The expenditure of one-pensioner and two-pensioner households is different from other households so separate indices have been compiled for pensioner households since 1968.

In 1979, the Conservative government introduced a new measure known as the Tax and Price Index (TPI) which has a broader coverage than the RPI. The RPI includes indirect taxes, but not direct taxes. The

Table 5.2 CSO press releases – subject areas

Overseas Trade (Balance of Payments) [m]
Retail Prices Index and Tax & Price Index [m]
Producer Prices [m]
Output of the Production Industries [m]
Cyclical Indicators [m]
Retail Sales [m]
Credit Business [m]
Vehicle Production [m]
Capital Expenditure (provisional & revised) [q]
Stocks (provisional & revised) [q]
Personal Income, Expenditure & Saving [q]
Consumer Expenditure [q]
GDP(O) [q]
GDP(O,I,E) [q]
Overseas Trade (Balance of Payments) [q]
Industrial & Commercial Companies [q]
Industry's Investment Intentions [twice a year]
Family Expenditure Survey [a]
Overseas Earnings of the City of London [a]
UK Official Reserves [m]*

m = monthly, q = quarterly, a = annual
* Published by the Treasury

TPI also covers direct taxes such as income tax and national insurance contributions. Changes in the TPI are based on price rises (including indirect taxes) and changes in direct taxes.

The TPI was introduced because the Thatcher government felt that the radical budget changes of 1979, with income tax cut from 33 to 30 per cent but VAT increased from 8 to 15 per cent, would not get a fair deal from the RPI. The VAT increases would push up the index but the income tax cuts would not be covered. The TPI was intended to present a broader picture, including both direct and indirect taxes. The TPI has failed to replace the RPI as the central measure of inflation and, although the TPI figure is still published, it receives little attention.

Two indexes of producer prices, previously known as wholesale prices and published since the 1950s, are produced monthly. One index covers the output of home sales of manufactured goods and another index covers input prices of materials and fuels purchased by manufacturing industry.

Economic growth is mainly measured by GDP statistics, although some other countries concentrate on GNP data which adds net property income from abroad to GDP. Official GDP statistics started to be collected during the Second World War but earlier estimates were produced by the Royal Economic Society. The existing series began in 1946 (annual) and 1955 (quarterly) for the expenditure and income estimates, and in 1948 (annual) and 1958 (quarterly) for the output estimates.

The figures are published quarterly and the first to appear are the GDP output statistics, usually published seven weeks after the quarter to which they relate. Approximately a month later, another press release is published covering the three measures of GDP plus GDP(A), an average of the three measures. The GDP output press release is largely based on the monthly *Output of the Production Industries* press release which is compiled from 330 separate indicators from different sectors of industry.

Near the end of every month, a press release is published relating to the balance of payments in the previous month. The statistics largely cover visible trade and a broader view of the balance of payments appears quarterly. This latter release is usually published two months after the quarter to which it relates.

The monthly *Cyclical Indicators* press release consists of four composite indicators and each of these is made up of a number of other indicators such as interest rates, retail sales, output and unemployment. The four indicators are the longer leading index, the shorter leading index, the coincident indicator and the lagging indicator.

Other official publications

The main economic and financial statistical publications are produced by the CSO, in collaboration with other government departments and the Bank of England. Economic forecasts are published by the Treasury.

Economic Trends

The monthly CSO publication, *Economic Trends*, is the standard statistical source for economic data. The first section, 'latest developments in the economy', is a short feature with the most up-to-date statistics on the previous month's economic trends. The main section in each issue consists of tables and charts of economic data, usually covering a number of recent months or quarters and recent full-year figures. A third section shows the movement of the cyclical indicators, described in the previous section, over a twenty-year period.

Quarterly articles on the national accounts appear in January, April, July and October and similar articles on the balance of payments are published in March, June, September and December. Data on individual cyclical indicators is published in February, May, August and November. Other articles are published occasionally.

Each issue has an alphabetical subject index and the release dates of forthcoming economic statistics are listed on the inside front cover. Press release data may be revised when it appears in *Economic Trends* and the statistics in *Economic Trends* itself may also be subject to revision. Major revisions to tables are usually announced at the beginning of each issue. *Economic Trends, Annual Supplement* provides the notes and definitions for the tables in the monthly issues plus historical tables, with data for up to 30 or 40 years, for some of the main indicators.

Financial Statistics

This is another monthly publication with statistics on the major financial indicators including financial accounts for various sectors of the economy, central government income and expenditure, local government and other public sector bodies, monetary sector, financial institutions and services, overseas sector, capital issues and stock exchange transactions, sector balance sheets, exchange rates, interest rates and security prices. The tables contain data for a number of months or quarters and years and each issue has an alphabetical subject index.

Financial Statistics, Explanatory Handbook is published annually with notes and definitions relating to the monthly tables and references for further information.

UK National Accounts: 'CSO Blue Book'

The *Blue Book*, published annually, is basically concerned with national and domestic income, production and current and capital expenditure. It also contains data on the UK's overseas surplus or deficit, the relationship of this to domestic production and expenditure and the flows of income, investment and finance between the UK and overseas. More detailed statistics on all these areas are given in the *Pink Book* described in the next paragraph.

The statistics give detailed estimates for the last ten years with summary data for the preceding ten-year period. The *Blue Book* revises a number of the quarterly estimates included in *Economic Trends*. An alphabetical subject index and brief notes are included in each issue. More detailed notes and definitions are published in *UK National Accounts, Sources and Methods* which was last published in 1985.

UK Balance of Payments: 'CSO Pink Book'

This is an annual publication with detailed balance of payments estimates for the latest ten years plus summary data for the preceding ten years. Numerous tables cover visible trade, invisibles, goods and services, while other sections cover transactions in UK external assets and liabilities, levels of UK external assets and liabilities, UK transactions with the EC and exchange rates.

The *Pink Book* often revises figures previously published in *Economic Trends* and press releases but some figures, particularly those relating to the latest years, are likely to be revised again when later and more complete information becomes available. The introduction to the *Pink Book* states that 'few of the estimates can be regarded as accurate to the nearest £ million'. An alphabetical subject index is included in each issue.

Other relevant CSO publications

Other CSO publications with some economic data are the *Annual Abstract of Statistics* and the *Monthly Digest of Statistics*. The annual *Regional Trends* contains some regional economic data. In 1989, the CSO launched a new series known as *Business Bulletins*. These bulletins, with individual titles on specific topics, appear regularly throughout the year and provide current statistics on key sectors of the economy. A list of the bulletins is given in the bibliography.

Treasury forecasts

The Treasury gives two annual forecasts of developments in the economy linked to the government's budget announcements. One is published on budget day, usually in March and is known as the *Financial Statement and Budget Report* and the other is the *Autumn Statement*.

An announcement in the March 1992 budget stated that this dual system of a budget in Spring and a public spending statement in Autumn will be abandoned. From 1993 onwards, the Autumn Statement and the Budget will be combined in one budget to take place in December each year and the publication of the Treasury forecasts will be linked to this budget.

Section 5 of the 1975 Industry Act requires the Treasury to publish two forecasts a year and the first *Autumn Statement* was published in December 1976. Treasury forecasts have been around a little longer with the first forecast published in 1947.

The budget forecast looks ahead to the middle of the following year and includes forecasts of GDP growth, retail price inflation, current account of the balance of payments, fixed investment, consumer spending, manufacturing output, exports and imports. The *Autumn Statement* concentrates on public spending plans and includes a section on the economic prospects for the coming year. The Treasury also publishes the margins of error attached to each forecast.

Various other forecasts are produced by non-official organizations and these are described in a later section of this chapter. *Forecasts of the UK Economy: a comparison of independent forecasts* is published monthly by the Treasury and contains basic figures from a selection of independent forecasters along with the Treasury forecast.

Other Treasury publications are *Economic Briefing*, published three times a year and available free of charge, and the *Treasury Bulletin* available on subscription. The former publication replaced the previously published *Economic Progress Report* and has brief items of economic news and statistics directed particularly at education users. The *Treasury Bulletin* has articles on economic issues plus accounts of economic policy and events. The first issue was published in Summer 1990.

CSO Databank

The CSO Databank contains most of the statistical series included in the publications described above. In publications such as *Economic Trends* and *Financial Trends*, the top of every column in a statistical table has a letter code and this is the letter code used for that statistical series in the databank.

The statistics on the databank are arranged in various 'datasets' corresponding to particular subject areas and a list of these is given in Table 5.3. The datasets are updated at monthly, quarterly or annual intervals depending on the frequency of the statistics. Datasets can be

Table 5.3 Datasets on the CSO Databank

Dataset	Frequency of Update
Economic Trends	monthly
National Accounts Quarterly Article	quarterly
Balance of Payments Quarterly Article	quarterly
*Index of Production, Cyclical Indicators and GDP(O)**	monthly
Employment and Earnings	monthly
RPI/TPI and Producer Price Indices	monthly
Financial Statistics and PSBR	monthly
Monthly Digest of Statistics	monthly
Consumers' Expenditure (disc only)	quarterly
UK Balance of Payments	annually
UK National Accounts	annually
Economic Trends Annual Supplement	annually

* GDP(O) dataset updated quarterly

supplied on tape or disc and on-line access to the data is available through a number of host bureaux including DRI, WEFA Group, Datastream International, IP Sharp and Scrimgeour Vickers. Details of these are given in Appendix 1.

CSO Statcall

The CSO offers a telephone service known as CSO Statcall and this covers the major economic statistics updated monthly: RPI, monthly trade figures, balance of payments (quarterly), PSBR, index of the output of the production industries, producer prices, retail sales, credit business and GDP. Calls are charged at 33p per minute cheap rate and 44p at other times. Details of the relevant telephone numbers for each series are given in Appendix 1.

CSO Statfax

From February 1992 onwards, anyone with a fax machine can obtain basic economic statistics on demand via their fax line. Economic statistics can be faxed by CSO within minutes of a press release being published. Further details are available from CSO.

Table 5.4 Bank of England press releases

Provisional Estimates of Monetary Aggregates (m)
Monetary Statistics (m)
Capital Issues and Redemptions (m)
London Sterling Certificates of Deposit (m)
Bill Turnover Statistics (m)
Sterling Commercial Paper (m)
Quarterly Analysis of Bank Advances (q)
Institutional Investment (q)
International Banking Statistics (q)

m = monthly, q = quarterly

Non-official statistics

Outside central government, major sources of economic and financial statistics are the Bank of England, the Stock Exchange, the Confederation of British Industry (CBI) and Chambers of Commerce. In addition, the importance attached to economic statistics is reflected in the number of organizations that publish regular reports commenting on and interpreting government economic data. These include the major banks with regular reviews of economic trends, stockbrokers, economic research institutes and academic institutions. The financial and business press, led by *The Financial Times*, is also a major source.

Bank of England and the financial sector

The bank's major publication is the *Bank of England Quarterly Bulletin* but it is also responsible for a group of press releases on the monetary and banking sector. Table 5.4 lists the key press releases produced by the Bank.

The monetary statistics are complicated because there is no single definition of money and there are many liquid assets which are not included in any of the UK monetary aggregates but which sometimes need to be taken into account when analysing monetary conditions. The result is a series of definitions of the money stock with statistics available based on all of these. The definitions most widely used are:

M0 is the narrowest measure of money, introduced in 1982. It consists of notes and coin in circulation outside the Bank of England and bankers' operational deposits at the Bank.

M2 also introduced in 1982, comprises notes and coins in circulation with the public plus sterling retail deposits held by the UK private sector with UK banks, building societies and in the National Savings Bank ordinary account.

M4 established in 1987, consists of notes and coins in circulation with the public, together with all sterling deposits (including certificates of deposit) held with UK banks and building societies by the rest of the private sector.

M5 also established in 1987, is equal to M4 plus private sector holdings of certain money market instruments, CTDs and some national savings instruments.

Apart from press releases, monetary statistics and figures on the financing of the Central Government Borrowing Requirement are published in the *Bank of England Quarterly Bulletin*. A commentary reviews trends in the domestic and international economy, the operations of monetary policy and financial market developments. Each issue also has a statistical annex with detailed data on the financial and banking sector. Notes and definitions accompany the statistics.

The range of statistics from the Bank are available via a magnetic tape service and long runs of data can be supplied in booklet form or on disc. The Bank's databank is also part of the on-line service offered by DRI Europe, and further details are given in the section on on-line databanks at the end of this chapter.

For a long time, the statistics published by the assortment of associations and other bodies in the financial services sector were fragmented and failed to keep pace with the dramatic changes in the sector. This is now changing and new series are being created to reflect the developments in the market.

This usually means that new series are unlikely to be comparable with previous series. For example, the British Bankers Association began a new set of banking statistics in May 1991 which include the newest bank, the Abbey National Group. This series replaced the previous statistics published by the Committee of London and Scottish Bankers although the two series are not comparable.

In the late 1980s, the growth in the range of institutions offering loans for house purchase was reflected in new industry-wide statistics published by the Council of Mortgage Lenders although individual building societies, banks and other institutions still publish statistics.

Other important publishers in the financial services sector are the Building Societies Association, Association of British Insurers, Association for Payment Clearing Services, the National Association of Pension Funds and the Unit Trust Association.

International Stock Exchange

Statistics from the Stock Exchange are essentially indicators of the performance in the UK equity market although additional statistics provide data on other areas such as the number and type of member companies. The *Quality of Markets Quarterly Review* has feature articles and a statistical annex with data on market values, new issues, turnover trends, traded options, the third market, member firms and the performance of other international stock markets. The *Quality of Markets Monthly Fact Sheet* shows trends in the key share indices, such as the FT Ordinary Share Index and the FT All-Share Index.

The All-Share Index was established in 1962 and covers 700 companies trading on the Stock Exchange. The total index is subdivided into 40 component indices covering specific industry groups and markets and, amongst the most important of these are the Industrial Group Index, 500 Share Index and the Financial Group Index. Changes in the indexes are calculated once a day and the figures are published in *The Financial Times* every day from Tuesday to Saturday. This index is more representative of the market as a whole than the other indexes but, because it is only calculated daily, it is slow to respond to market changes.

The FT Ordinary Share Index, or the FT Index, was established in 1935 and it is based on the 30 largest independent UK companies. Originally, changes were calculated daily then hourly and now its continuous movements are recorded. Its closing daily value appears on the front page of the next day's *Financial Times* and its hourly movements, movements over the past week, its level a year ago and its highs and lows are published in an FT table headed 'Financial Times Stock Indices'. This index is well established, going back to 1935, and it is easy and quick to calculate. It should also be sensitive to changes in the financial market as it is based on the shares of heavily traded 'blue chip' companies. Its weaknesses are that it is unlikely to be representative of British industry as a whole and it is unweighted which means that dramatic changes in the share values of one company can have an exaggerated effect on the index as a whole.

In 1984, the FT Ordinary Share Index was only updated hourly but the demands of the market required an index which could show continuous changes. So the FT-SE 100 Share Index was established, updated every minute between 8.30 in the morning and 4.00 in the afternoon on a normal working day. The FT-SE 100 Share Index, or the 'Footsie' as it is popularly known, is calculated by computer and is a real-time measure of performance based on the top 100 UK companies according to market capitalization.

The qualification for admission on the first day of its operation was a market value of just under £300 million but, by the end of 1990, this had risen to around £1 billion. Changes in company fortunes mean that a handful of companies are forced to leave the Footsie each year while new ones join from the All-Share Index to take their place. A company is usually replaced if it has fallen below 110 in the pecking order and if a replacement company has moved into the top 90. Of the 100 companies that made up the original index in 1984, 72 were still there at the end of 1990.

The index is a weighted arithmetic index and the change in price of a company share is weighted according to that company's issued share capital. This means that price movements in the shares of the 100th company will have less effect on the index than price movements relating to the top companies.

Other specialist indices published in *The Financial Times* are the Government Securities Index, which charts the progress of a representative cross-section of gilt-edged stocks, the Fixed Interest Index, and the Gold Mines Index based on the performance of 24 South African mines. Every week, all the UK financial market statistics listed in the daily *Financial Times* are published on a microfiche known as the *FT Stats Fiche* and published by McCarthy. Publications from the FT Business Research Centre include *FT Monthly Stock Indices*, with daily information on all the major indexes plus highs, lows and averages for the month, *Quarterly FT Actuaries Indices* and *FT Monthly Currency Statistics and World Stock Indices*.

Confederation of British Industry (CBI)

The CBI's monthly *Economic Situation Report* gives a general economic survey plus short term forecasts of the economy. Extracts from all the other regular CBI surveys are also included and these surveys are listed in Chapter 6. Regional economic information is published in a relatively new title, *Regional Trends Survey* published quarterly. The title is jointly produced with Business Strategies Ltd (BSL) which carries out research on regional economies.

Association of British Chambers of Commerce (ABCC)

Individual Chambers of Commerce around the country have been publishing economic surveys of their areas for many years but in 1985, the ABCC started to publish a national survey based on the results of 13 individual surveys carried out in different parts of the country. The *British Chambers of Commerce Quarterly Economic Survey* is based on the regular responses from member companies.

Company executives are asked to show the trends in key indicators affecting their business in the current quarter and to offer an opinion on the likely trends in the coming quarter. Indicators covered include home orders and deliveries, exports, employment, investment, business confidence and capacity utilization. The 13 regional offices supplying data are located in the North East, North West, Merseyside, Yorkshire and Humberside, East Midlands, West Midlands, Wales, Northern Ireland, East Anglia, Thames Valley, Home Counties North, South West, and London.

The survey includes data on services as well as manufacturing and, by providing data at a regional level, it can show how specific geographical areas are responding to periods of economic growth or recession.

Economic forecasting organizations

There are at least 35 organizations in the UK publishing regular forecasts of the UK economy. There are also forecasts from the major international organizations notably the Organization for Economic Co-operation and Development (OECD), Commission of the European Communities and the International Monetary Fund (IMF).

These forecasts provide an indication of likely changes to key economic variables in the future and may be used by many organizations in the form in which they are published or may be incorporated into specific internal forecasts compiled by particular companies. Forecasting publications typically contain forecasts of future trends, estimates of trends in the recent past, historical data and an interpretation of this data and trends.

Forecasts for the UK Economy published monthly by the Treasury

Table 5.5 Selected UK-based forecasting organizations

Cambridge Econometrics
Confederation of British Industry (CBI)
Data Resources Inc (DRI)
Henley Centre
National Institute of Economic and Social Research (NIESR)
WEFA Group

Oxford University (Oxford Economic Forecasting)
Liverpool University (Liverpool Research Group in Macroeconomics)
London Business School (LBS)

National Westminster Bank plc
Barclays Bank plc

Goldman Sachs
Hoare Govett
Philips & Drew
County Nat West
James Capel
Greenwell Montague
Barclays de Zoete Wedd
S G Warburg Securities
Shearson Lehman
Morgan Grenfell
Credit Lyonnais/Laing & Cruikshank
Williams de Broe

compares the forecasts from a selection of forecasters. A list of the UK forecasters regularly monitored is given in Table 5.5. These include independent research organizations, academic institutions, banks and stockbrokers.

The majority of forecasts are based on econometric models which were developed in the USA in the 1930s but were only generally used in the UK in the 1960s. In econometric forecasting, a series of equations is used to model the economy and these models are regularly reviewed and refined. The models use existing data to produce estimates and forecasts with the resulting figures often being amended by, or supplemented with, the judgements of the particular forecaster.

In 1961, the National Institute of Economic and Social Research began publishing forecasts and, in 1966, the London Business School's forecasts were established. Later in the 1970s the real growth in UK forecasting took place as many organizations tried to deal with the economic consequences of the oil shocks of 1973 and 1979.

The forecasts that exist today are based on a variety of models and a wide range of assumptions. Individual forecasts may cover different time periods and give weight to different economic indicators.

Each forecast makes assumptions about the factors affecting economic change and these assumptions fashion the nature of the forecast that is produced. At one end are the strong monetarist models, exemplified by the Liverpool University forecast. At the other end are the Keynesian models, pioneered by the National Institute of Economic Research, which assume that money and supply-side factors play a relatively minor role in the economy and that other variables play a more significant role.

Short-term forecasts generally cover the next 12 to 18 months and the majority of forecasts produced by stockbrokers fall into this category. Medium-term forecasts usually give figures up to five years ahead and, beyond this, forecasts become long term. Forecasts can look at the changes in absolute values of economic variables or measure the rate of change in these variables.

Macro-economic forecasts cover the major economic variables such as inflation, economic growth (GDP), balance of payments, consumer spending and unemployment although some forecasting organizations have reputations as strong forecasters of particular economic variables. A specialist branch of forecasting has built up around the prediction of exchange rate changes while disaggregated forecasts are available for particular sectors of the economy and specific regions of the country.

Choosing the appropriate forecast, or a combination of forecasts, for a particular circumstance may require a detailed look at the characteristics, assumptions and track records of specific forecasting organizations. A general guide to the various UK forecasts, with comments from users of UK forecasts, is included in the *World Index of Economic Forecasts* published by Gower. Detailed information on the models, databases and forecasts produced by a selection of UK forecasters is held at the Macroeconomic Modelling Bureau, established by the ESRC in 1983 at the University of Warwick.

Local economic data

Some local authorities publish regular economic reviews of their area although most of these are based on an analysis of central government data. In the 1980s, authorities of all political persuasions recognized that they could play an important role in the regeneration of their local economies and many established economic development units, enterprise boards and industrial development agencies. These units gave some impetus to the collection of local economic data and many are producing regular economic statistics, economic development plans and employment plans. Local chambers of commerce often carry out economic surveys like the London Chamber of Commerce's quarterly *Economic Report and Survey*.

Independent companies offering economic information for regions and local areas across the UK include Cambridge Econometrics, Business Strategies Ltd and the Reward Group with its main publication, *Cost of Living Report – Regional Comparisons*, published three times a year. It shows cost of living trends in 100 towns and cities in the UK. Property consultants and developers such as Debenham Tewson & Chinnocks, Healey & Baker, Drivers Jonas, Jones Lang Wooton and Hillier Parker can give an indication of the economic buoyancy of an area through their regular surveys of industrial and commercial values and rents.

A growing group of publications on local economies comes from local business schools and academic institutions with reports often based on a survey of businesses in a particular area. Some examples include the *Welsh Economic Review*, published twice a year by Cardiff Business School, the quarterly *Scottish Business Survey* from the University of Strathclyde, the *East Midlands Business Survey* from Nottingham Business School and the *West Midlands Business Survey* from Wolverhampton Polytechnic. The latter is published in association with Price Waterhouse and this link between an academic institution and a private organization reflects a growing trend with this type of publication.

Alternative economic indicators

The debate on the accuracy of official economic statistics has led to some non-official alternatives to the official figures. Examples are the

Sunday Times/Institute for Fiscal Studies (IFS) retail price index and the Low Paid Price Index produced by the Low Pay Unit and the NUCPS civil service union. The latter index measures monthly changes in the standard of living for households with a gross income of £125 to £150 a week (at June 1990).

The *Sunday Times*/IFS index was launched as an alternative to the official RPI in June 1990 because it was felt that the official index failed to measure housing costs accurately. The new index is updated monthly and is published just after the release of the official RPI. The official RPI includes mortgage interest payments as the main element of an owner occupier's housing costs.

The calculation of housing costs in the new index is based on the principle that housing is an investment asset which produces a return for its owner. Mortgage payments are therefore balanced by the capital gains accruing to home owners.

There are still costs associated with owner occupation and the new index identifies two elements which are included in the calculation of the index. The first is a depreciation charge, which is a fixed percentage of the value of the housing stock, and so varies with the level of house prices. The second is the net cost of borrowing for house purchase, in relation to the return on saving, and is measured as the difference between mortgage rates and typical bank and building society deposit rates.

The *Sunday Times*/Institute for Fiscal Studies index gives a much greater weight to house prices than does the official index and this is considered appropriate because house prices are a major indicator of inflationary pressure. Interest rates, included in the official index, have less influence on the new index. The poll tax is also included in the official index but excluded from the non-official alternative.

A number of non-official organizations also publish regular statistics on house prices and, given the important role these prices play in the inflationary process, they have become important economic indicators. An article on house prices in the November 1984 issue of the *National Westminster Bank Quarterly Review* identified over 20 regular sources of house price data, usually published monthly or quarterly and covering national prices and prices in specific regions and towns. These sources range from individual building societies and banks such as the Halifax, Nationwide, Abbey National and Woolwich through to industry bodies like the Building Societies Association and the Council of Mortgage Lenders and professional associations such as the Royal Institution of Chartered Surveyors.

The diversity of sources available and the different methods they use to calculate house price changes can produce confusing and conflicting statistics. The main problem revolves around the fact that few houses are actually identical, with most properties having clear physical differences, different locations and different environments. Any measure of house prices based on a particular group of properties is unlikely to be the same as a measure based on another group and the mix of properties in one particular group is likely to change over time. The result is that no national composite measure of house prices exists and it is difficult to compare one source's figures with another as the examples described below will show.

Statistics from building societies, like the Halifax and Nationwide are based on the individual society's mortgage approvals. The figures are usually weighted to take account of the mix of properties covered by their surveys and the changes in the mix from one survey period to another.

House price data published by the Building Societies Association is based on a much larger sample with survey returns covering 80 per cent to 85 per cent of building society mortgage advances but the figures are not adjusted to reflect changes in the mix of properties. Data on regional prices is based on only a 5 per cent sample survey. Figures from the Royal Institute of Chartered Surveyors come from an analysis of the comments made by local estate agents.

On-line databanks

Although many statistics are still unavailable through on-line sources, on-line databanks containing economic and financial data are relatively well developed. Most of the on-line sources are available through host computer bureaux offering access to a number of databases. The major bureaux are international organizations with offices in the UK and they offer access to databases produced by national statistical offices such as the CSO, by central banks like the Bank of England or by international bodies such as the European Commission, Organization for Economic Co-operation and Development or the International Monetary Fund. Contact information is given in the Appendix and brief details of the major services are given below.

A major international supplier of on-line economic data is DRI (Data Resources Inc) which has a number of databases including DRI

Europe, DRI Current Economic Indicators and DRI European Forecast. The databases incorporate data from a number of sources including national statistical offices and international organizations. Files can be updated weekly, daily or monthly. The CSO Databank and the Bank of England database are part of DRI's databases. The company also produces databases on specific economic sectors, commodities and international trade.

Datastream International is largely known for its company information databases but it also provides on-line access to data on economic indicators, economic forecasts and securities. The files are continuously updated by the company. The CSO Databank is part of the company's service.

Other host systems offering economic data include the WEFA Group and I P Sharp. Both are agents for the CSO Databank and both provide access to other international economic and financial databases.

Finstat is produced by *The Financial Times* and is available on-line via Telecom Gold. A section of the database covers the FT Indices and other sections cover securities, gilts, unit trusts, insurance funds and offshore funds. Updating is carried out daily.

Real time information services provide real time price information for shares. These services can be screen-based or telephone-based. They give share price information on individual stocks and most will also give general information on financial trends and changes to the major share indices. The number of such services has grown in recent years although some of the newly established telephone services have failed to take off and have subsequently been dropped. Some of the main services are described here.

Topic is the International Stock Exchange's own financial information system, based on videotex technology. Users can access Topic via a stand-alone terminal or through a computer-to-computer link and there is a PC-based version. Cityservice is a videotex service produced by British Telecom with data on international market prices. Citywatch, another screen-based service from Reuters Ltd, gives access to key prices from the foreign exchange, money and futures markets in Europe, North America and Asia.

6 Business Statistics

Statistics on specific UK industries and sectors, and products and services within these sectors, appear in a range of publications from official and non-official sources. At a general level, business statistics provide information on the structure of a particular sector or group of sectors with data on areas such as the number of companies or establishments, the size of companies or establishments, output, turnover, sales or value-added, purchases, sector employment and wages, trade, investment and general financial performance. At a more detailed level, there may be information on areas such as the sales, production, trade and deliveries of specific products and services.

Over the last 100 years, manufacturing has been at the centre of the country's economic development and the published business statistics reflect this with a strong emphasis on data on particular manufacturing sectors. The major official series is the *Census of Production*, which began at the beginning of the century, and has annual data on specific industries. The major source of information on the sales of particular manufactured products and UK trade in these products is a series of regular *Business Monitor* reports started in the 1960s.

Other traditionally important sectors, notably agriculture, forestry and fishing, mining, construction, energy and transport are also covered relatively well. In contrast, published statistics on the growing services sector are relatively new and still limited although, in recent years, some attempt has been made to improve the official series in this area and more non-official sources have emerged.

The numerous business sectors in the UK are arranged logically in a classification scheme known as the Standard Industrial Classification (SIC) and most of the official publications, and many of the non-official series, base their statistics on this classification. This UK classification should not be confused with the US SIC which uses a totally different classification method and is used by one or two organizations in this country, notably Dun & Bradstreet. Before describing the key publications, a description of the UK SIC is given in the next section of this chapter.

To complicate matters for the user, not all series are based on this classification and other systems include the VAT Trade Classification (VTC), used particularly in some statistical series on the service industries, and the Standard International Trade Classification (SITC) and the Harmonised Commodity Description and Coding System (HS), both of which are used with import and export statistics. All these classifications are described in later sections of this chapter.

The Standard Industrial Classification (SIC)

The Standard Industrial Classification (SIC) is a classification system of economic activity in the UK, including the production industries, energy, construction, services and agriculture, forestry and fishing. It attempts to reflect the organization and structure of industry in the UK and it is updated at regular intervals to incorporate any changes in industrial structure and characteristics.

The first SIC was published in 1948 and there were revisions in 1958 and 1968. The current classification is the SIC (1980) Revised which has been in use from 1983. It is an attempt to align the UK classification with another classification used by the Statistical Office of the European Communities. This classification is known as the General Industrial Classification of Economic Activities within the EC, usually abbreviated to NACE. There is still little widespread use of NACE across EC countries but, in October 1990, the EC members agreed to establish a common classification of economic activities thus opening the way for the development of the NACE system. A new NACE classification will be produced in the early 1990s, known as NACE Rev 1, and a revised UK SIC is also planned.

Table 6.1 SIC (1980) Revised divisions

0	Agriculture, Forestry & Fishing
1	Energy & Water Supply Industries
2	Extraction of Minerals & Ores other than Fuels; Manufacture of Metals, Mineral Products & Chemicals
3	Metal Goods, Engineering & Vehicles Industries
4	Other Manufacturing Industries
5	Construction
6	Distribution, Hotels & Catering; Repairs
7	Transport and Communication
8	Banking, Finance, Insurance, Business Services & Leasing
9	Other Services

Table 6.2 UK SIC – examples of subdivisions from Division 4

Division 4	Other Manufacturing
subdivided into, for example:	
Class 41	Food, Drink & Tobacco Manufacturing Industries
Group 419	Bread, Biscuits & Flour Confectionery
Activity Heading 4196	Bread & Flour Confectionery
Activity Heading 4197	Biscuits & Crispbread

The current UK SIC is made up of ten general divisions, listed in Table 6.1, and these divisions are divided into 60 classes, 222 groups and 334 activity headings. Each of these subdivisions of the classification is given a number code and these codes become larger as the sector becomes more specific. For example, division 4 is 'Other Manufacturing' but this is then broken down into various subdivisions with two, three or four digit codes as Table 6.2 shows.

Sectors identified by the three digit code form the basis of the published output for the Census of Production. Activity headings, with four digits, are used as the basis for the annual and quarterly

Business Monitor production series containing data on specific product areas.

Industry and product statistics are the responsibility of the CSO's office at Newport, previously known as the Business Statistics Office (BSO). A register of businesses in the UK is held at the CSO and this forms the framework for the enquiries to the production sector. For firms in the construction sector, a register of businesses is produced annually from the Department of Environment's Builders Address File.

Official statistics

Sector information: Census of Production

A regular survey of the organization and structure of industry in the UK is the Census of Production which is currently undertaken annually. It is a statutory inquiry under the Statistics of Trade Act 1947 and is based on returns from industrial and construction companies. The census covers divisions 1 to 5 of the SIC and, as its name suggests, it does not cover agriculture, forestry or fishing or the service sectors covered by divisions 6 to 9 of the SIC.

Central government uses the census data to produce weights for the index of production and to provide capital expenditure and stocks data for use in compiling the national accounts. Results are also used as a benchmark for the Purchases Inquiry, described later in this chapter, as well as for information on industrial structure, which is used to assess various policy issues.

Specifically, it provides information on numbers and sizes of companies, employment, output, costs, capital expenditure, stocks, work in progress and operating ratios for various sectors and for industry in total. Most of the information collected can be analysed by size of business and, in some cases, by region.

The first production census was in 1907 and, from 1907 to 1968, a detailed census was carried out approximately every five years with one or two exceptions. In between the detailed censuses, simple censuses or interim censuses were undertaken. In 1970, some of the detailed information contained in earlier censuses was taken over by other surveys: detailed information on commodity purchases and product sales, for example, was covered by other surveys.

In 1980, a new series of annual censuses was introduced. Starting in 1980, 'slimline' censuses have been carried out in most years with a more substantial 'benchmark' census every five years. The first benchmark inquiry covered 1984. The slimline censuses were introduced to reduce the form-filling burden on the business community but, in turn, the amount of information collected in these censuses has also been reduced.

The increased use of sampling in recent years has led to a gradual fall in the number of firms mailed. For the production industries, excluding construction, the forms mailed have fallen from 34 000 in 1977 to 16 128 in 1987 and 16 050 in 1988. In the construction industries, the number of forms mailed fell from 13 000 in 1977 to 6 100 in 1984 and 4 225 in 1988.

For the 1988 census, in the production industries, forms were sent to all businesses with 100 or more employees. A 1 in 2 sample was used, for most industries, for businesses in the 50 to 99 employment size band and a 1 in 4 sample was used for businesses in the 20 to 49 employment size band. In the construction sector, forms were mailed to all companies with 50 or more employees and to a 1 in 2 sample for companies with between 20 and 49 employees.

The sampling scheme and methods are reviewed each year and, in each year's census, estimates are made for non-respondents, unsatisfactory returns and businesses not selected including companies employing less than 20 people. Forms are mailed to various businesses shortly after the end of the year to which the census relates and returns are required within a few months.

The processing and analysis of the results takes time and published information from the census does not start to appear until approximately 12 to 15 months after the census has taken place. Results from the 1988 census, for example, started to be published at the beginning of 1990.

The results are published in a series known as the *Business Monitor PA Series* starting with *Business Monitor PA 1001*, an introductory volume with notes and descriptions of the census. There are 113 industry volumes corresponding to the groups of the SIC and a list of these reports is given in Table 6.3. The reports are published gradually over a period of time and the last report to appear is usually *Business Monitor PA 1002*, a summary volume giving basic information for the industry sector in total and comparative information for specific sectors.

Census results for Northern Ireland are included in the reports but the Department of Economic Development in Northern Ireland also

Table 6.3 Census of Production reports

PA1001	Introductory notes
PA111	Coal extraction and manufacture of solid fuels
PA120	Coke ovens
PA130	Extraction of mineral oil and natural gas
PA140	Mineral oil processing
PA161	Production and distribution of electricity
PA162	Public gas supply
PA170	Water supply industry
PA221	Iron and steel industry
PA222	Steel tubes
PA223	Drawing, cold rolling and cold forming of steel
PA224	Non-ferrous metals industry
PA231	Extraction of stone, clay, sand and gravel
PA239	Extraction of miscellaneous minerals (including salt)
PA241	Structural clay products
PA242	Cement, lime and plaster
PA243	Building products of concrete, cement and plaster
PA244	Asbestos goods
PA245	Working of stone and other non-metallic minerals
PA246	Abrasive products
PA247	Glass and glassware
PA248	Refractory and ceramic goods
PA251	Basic industrial chemicals
PA255	Paints, varnishes and printing ink
PA256	Specialised chemical products mainly for industrial and agricultural purposes
PA257	Pharmaceutical products
PA258	Soap and toilet preparations
PA259	Specialised chemical products mainly for household and office use
PA260	Production of man-made fibres
PA311	Foundries
PA312	Forging, pressing and stamping
PA313	Bolts, nuts, etc.; springs; non-precision chains; metals treatment
PA314	Metal doors, windows, etc.
PA316	Hand tools and finished metal goods
PA320	Industrial plant and steelwork
PA321	Agricultural machinery and tractors
PA322	Metal-working machine tools and engineers' tools
PA323	Textile machinery
PA324	Machinery for the food, chemical and related industries; process engineering contractors

Table 6.3 continued

PA325	Mining machinery, construction and mechanical handling equipment
PA326	Mechanical power transmission equipment
PA327	Machinery for printing, wood, leather, rubber, glass and related industries: laundry and dry cleaning machinery
PA328	Miscellaneous machinery and mechanical equipment
PA329	Ordnance, small arms and ammunition
PA330	Manufacture of office machinery and data processing equipment
PA341	Insulated wires and cables
PA342	Basic electrical equipment
PA343	Electrical equipment for industrial use, and batteries and accumulators
PA344	Telecommunication equipment, electrical measuring equipment, electronic capital goods and passive electronic components
PA345	Miscellaneous electronic equipment
PA346	Domestic-type electric appliances
PA347	Electric lamps and other electric lighting equipment
PA351	Motor vehicles and their engines
PA352	Motor vehicle bodies, trailers and caravans
PA353	Motor vehicle parts
PA361	Shipbuilding and repairing
PA362	Railway and tramway vehicles
PA363	Cycles and motorcycles
PA364	Aerospace equipment manufacturing and repairing
PA365	Miscellaneous vehicles
PA371	Measuring, checking and precision instruments and apparatus
PA372	Medical and surgical equipment and orthopaedic appliances
PA373	Optical precision instruments and photographic equipment
PA374	Clocks, watches and other timing devices
PA411	Organic oils and fats
PA412	Slaughtering of animals and production of meat and by-products
PA413	Preparation of milk and milk products
PA414	Processing of fruit and vegetables
PA415	Fish processing
PA416	Grain milling
PA419	Bread, biscuits and flour confectionery
PA420	Sugar and sugar by-products
PA421	Ice-cream, cocoa, chocolate and sugar confectionery
PA422	Animal feeding stuffs

Table 6.3 concluded

PA423	Starch and miscellaneous foods
PA424	Spirit distilling and compounding
PA426	Wines, cider and perry
PA427	Brewing and malting
PA428	Soft drinks
PA429	Tobacco industry
PA431	Woollen and worsted industry
PA432	Cotton and silk industries
PA433	Throwing, texturing, etc. of continuous filament yarn
PA434	Spinning and weaving of flax, hemp and ramie
PA435	Jute and polypropylene yarns and fabrics
PA436	Hosiery and other knitted goods
PA437	Textile finishing
PA438	Carpets and other textile floorcoverings
PA439	Miscellaneous textiles
PA441	Leather (tanning and dressing) and fellmongery
PA442	Leather goods
PA451	Footwear
PA453	Clothing, hats and gloves
PA455	Household textiles and other made-up textiles
PA456	Fur goods
PA461	Sawmilling, planing, etc. of wood
PA462	Manufacture of semi-finished wood products and further processing and treatment of wood
PA463	Builders' carpentry and joinery
PA464	Wooden containers
PA465	Miscellaneous wooden articles
PA466	Articles of cork and plaiting materials, brushes and brooms
PA467	Wooden and upholstered furniture and shop and office fittings
PA471	Pulp, paper and board
PA472	Conversion of paper and board
PA475	Printing and publishing
PA481	Rubber products
PA483	Processing of plastics
PA491	Jewellery and coins
PA492	Musical instruments
PA493	Photographic and cinematographic processing laboratories
PA494	Toys and sports goods
PA495	Miscellaneous manufacturing industries
PA500	Construction
PA1002	Summary volume

Source: HMSO

publishes separate annual results for Northern Ireland. These reports are similar to the UK reports but contain additional information on wages, salaries and energy purchases.

More detailed information from the census is available, for a fee, from the CSO in Newport.

Although the census is a statutory inquiry, and non-respondents are chased up, lack of response is still a problem. In other cases, companies have responded but these responses are unsatisfactory and they are not included in the published results. Government statistics are also not allowed to divulge information on specific companies and this confidentiality rule may affect the production of aggregate statistics on a particular sector.

A combination of all these factors means that coverage of the eventual published data can vary considerably from industry to industry. A footnote to the first table in each industry report gives an indication of the resulting industry coverage. The 1988 industry report *PA 420 Sugar and sugar by-products* states that satisfactory returns accounted for 97 per cent of employment within the industry but this is a high percentage compared to most industry reports. In *PA 483 Processing of plastics*, for example, the percentage is 67 per cent and in *PA 465 Miscellaneous wooden articles*, the percentage is only 38 per cent.

Revisions to the SIC, and changes in the detail and format of the census over time make it difficult to compare recent censuses with earlier ones while the specific questions asked can also vary from census to census. The 1984 benchmark census included a question on road transport costs and postal and telecommunications costs but this question has not been asked since. In 1988, 1987, and 1986, additional questions were asked on the number of computer employees, costs of computer equipment purchased and, for larger businesses only, costs of hiring, leasing or renting computer equipment and the amounts paid for computer services. Other additional questions in 1988 covered the costs of assets leased under finance leasing agreements.

Major sectors

While the Census of Production is the major source of information on the structure of economic activity in this country, information on key sectors can be obtained from other publications. Figures produced by the Department of Environment (DoE) cover the construction industries. Data on the agricultural sector, which is excluded from the Census of Production, come from the Ministry of Agriculture,

Fisheries & Foods (MAFF). Other publications cover transport and energy sectors.

Construction

Housing and Construction Statistics is an annual publication with statistics on the construction sector over a ten-year period.

One section covers the structure of the industry including data on the number of private contractors, employment, work done, number of firms by size and region and employment trends by firm size. Data on the number of private contractors are broken down by type of contractor. This information is obtained through forms sent to companies on the DoE's register of private contracting firms. Statistics are also available on local authority and new town building departments. Other sections cover orders and output, labour, materials, investment and housing.

Some of these statistics are updated in a quarterly publication also known as *Housing and Construction Statistics* which is published in two parts each quarter. Indicators of short-term trends in the sector come from various press notices available from the department. Monthly press notices cover housebuilding, construction new orders, building new orders, building materials and components, brick production and new orders by type of work. Quarterly notices relate to construction output and employment, planning applications and decisions, renovations and homeless households. An annual press notice is titled slum clearance.

Agriculture

Agricultural Statistics UK is an annual publication which includes the main figures from the annual agricultural census. Various tables cover the number of agricultural holdings, size of holdings and distribution by tenure and type of activity. Other tables cover the employment structure and specific sections provide information by county and information on the horticulture sector.

Separate publications are available for Scotland, Wales and Northern Ireland: *Economic Report on Scottish Agriculture* (Scottish Office); *Welsh Agricultural Statistics* (Welsh Office); *Statistical Review of Northern Ireland Agriculture* (Department of Agriculture for Northern Ireland). Other publications covering the structure of the agriculture sector are *Annual Review of Agriculture and Agriculture in the UK*, both published annually.

Transport

Transport Statistics Great Britain is an annual statistical review of transport trends, including some data on the structure of the sector. *Quarterly Transport Statistics* is one of a series of regular bulletins available from the Department of Transport. Various other regular statistical publications cover areas such as traffic, heavy goods vehicles, roads, accidents and new registrations and a list of these is included at the back of *Transport Statistics Great Britain*.

Energy

The annual *Digest of UK Energy Statistics* contains tables and charts on the UK energy sector, with specific sections on particular types of energy. The monthly *Energy Trends*, available from the Department of Energy, has basic data on energy consumption, production and prices. A monthly press notice gives *Advance Energy Statistics*.

VAT records

General details on the number and sizes of companies are also available from VAT records. Companies registering for VAT are categorized into a particular trade based on the VAT Trade Classification (VTC). This classification is similar to the SIC 1968, except that its breakdown for service and distributive trades is more detailed than the SIC, but it is not comparable with the SIC (1980) Revised.

Basic statistics on the number and size of companies registered for VAT, new registrations and de-registrations are published regularly in the *Employment Gazette*. More detailed information, by local authority districts in Great Britain and industry groups for the English and Welsh counties and Scottish regions are available, for a fee, from the Department of Employment.

The annual *Business Monitor PA 1003 Size Analysis of UK Businesses* contains statistics, based on VAT records, on the number of UK businesses in total and breakdowns by turnover, business types, SIC activity headings and classes, employment size and regions and counties. The *Annual Report of HM Customs and Excise* also has basic VAT statistics.

Statistics based on VAT records include all businesses and not just those in the production sector. They are also based on all companies registered for VAT and not just a sample.

As a measure of industry sizes and trends, the VAT statistics are useful but they have certain limitations. First, a new VAT registration does not necessarily mean the birth of a new company. An existing firm may have just reached the VAT threshold or become part of a larger group. Many small firms are not registered for VAT so estimates of numbers in specific sectors and local areas must be treated with caution. In 1986, for example, it was estimated that 1 million companies were not registered for VAT. New registrations and de-registrations may take some time to appear on the VAT database and changes in the VAT threshold, like the large jump in the minimum turnover threshold announced in the 1991 budget, will also affect registration trends.

Other sources

The Purchases Inquiry is undertaken every five years and gives broad commodity details of industry's purchases of materials and fuels. The 1984 Inquiry covered the purchases of 10 000 of the UK's largest companies but the collection of this information is particularly burdensome. The sample size and detail is likely to be reduced in future inquiries.

Companies in 199– is published annually by the DTI and gives the numbers and new registrations of public and private companies in Great Britain. In Northern Ireland, the same information is included in the *Companies General Annual Report*. The latter source also includes information on company liquidations in Northern Ireland and the *Companies General Annual Report* for Great Britain has similar information.

Service sectors

Distribution

The first census of distribution was in 1950 and from 1950 to 1971, large scale comprehensive censuses of distribution were undertaken at periodic intervals. Thus 1957, 1961 and 1971 were full census years with sample censuses in 1957 and 1966. The extensive results of the 1971 census were published in thirteen volumes. All these censuses covered both retailing and wholesaling but, in the 1970s and 1980s, separate retailing and wholesaling inquiries were developed.

Retailing

In 1976, the comprehensive surveys of distribution were replaced by a new series of sample inquiries into retailing which contained less information but appeared much more frequently. From 1976 to 1980, these surveys were annual and then they were carried out every other year in 1982, 1984 and 1986. In 1987, a further change occurred when a new style of 'intermediate' retail inquiry was undertaken for the first time. These intermediate inquiries are now carried out annually except for every fifth year when a full retail inquiry is undertaken. (A full inquiry was carried out in 1990.)

Certain intermediate inquiries will be deemed 'enhanced intermediate' inquiries and these will have additional information on specific commodity headings. Intermediate inquiries collect limited commodity information under 16 headings but the enhanced intermediate inquiries will cover 41 headings.

The retail inquiry collects data on stocks, capital expenditure, total turnover, retail turnover, a breakdown of commodity sales, retail sales by special forms of trading, purchases, outlets and employment. In the 1987 inquiry, additional questions were asked on the expenditure on computer acquisitions and associated computer personnel.

The results of the inquiry are published in *Business Monitor SDA 25 Retailing*, sometimes referred to as the 'retail inquiry'. This publication appears many months after the inquiry itself: the results of the 1987 inquiry, for example, were published in 1990.

The inquiry is based on a sample of businesses in Great Britain obtained from a register of legal units held by the CSO at Newport which in turn is maintained from information supplied from VAT records. In the 1987 inquiry, the sample comprised 12 000 businesses and the response rate was 81 per cent.

All businesses with a turnover of £2 million or more were included in the sample and, immediately below this level, the sampling rate was 2 in 5 falling to 1 in 53 for the smallest businesses included in the sample. No independent retail business with a turnover of less than £44 000 was sent a form but estimates were made for this sector. Estimates were also made for non-respondents and for voluntary VAT registrations below the VAT threshold.

The inquiry excludes businesses not registered for VAT because they are considered to be too small: there are believed to be approximately 30 000 businesses in this category but these account for a very small percentage of total retail sales at around 0.5 per cent.

The current VAT classification, which forms the basis of the retail inquiry, is closely aligned to the 1968 SIC but not the latest SIC, revised in 1980. This means that certain sectors, such as hire and repair businesses, which are no longer allocated to retailing in the new SIC are still covered in the retail inquiry. Conversely, petrol filling stations and the retail distribution of motor vehicles and accessories, which are now part of retailing in the latest SIC, are not covered. These are included in a separate inquiry on the motor trades.

From 1986, the inquiry basically collects data from businesses whose main activity is retailing and only a limited amount of information comes from businesses engaged in retailing as a subsidiary activity. Previously, more information was collected from these businesses where retailing is a subsidiary activity.

This has led to a discontinuity in the series, with figures from 1984 and earlier not strictly comparable with figures in 1986 and onwards. The 1986 published survey includes 1980, 1982 and 1984 figures re-worked onto the same basis as those for 1986.

Wholesaling

Since 1950, wholesaling has been included in the occasional comprehensive censuses of distribution. In 1959 and 1965, simple wholesale inquiries were carried out. From 1965 onwards, there were smaller sample inquiries to collect information on stocks and expenditure. A relatively detailed Wholesaling and Dealing Inquiry was undertaken in 1974: this inquiry was postponed for a year so that it could be the first inquiry to use the register of businesses based on VAT classifications which was established in 1973.

From 1980 onwards, there have been annual wholesaling inquiries collecting regular data on total turnover, beginning- and end-year total stocks, and capital expenditure with certain rotating topics covered in selected years. In the 1988 inquiry, specific questions covered the amount of capital expenditure incurred by lessees on assets leased on a finance lease basis. The basic results of the survey are published annually in *Business Monitor SDA 26 Wholesaling*.

In addition to businesses engaged in traditional wholesaling operations, like buying from manufacturers and selling to retailers, the inquiry also includes companies involved in other areas such as operational leasing, commodity broking, factoring and importing and exporting. Businesses carrying out wholesaling as a subsidiary activity are not included.

For the 1988 survey, a random sample of 8 300 businesses from the register of legal units was selected and the results are based on a response rate of 91 per cent of the total number of forms sent out. No independent wholesaling business with a VAT turnover of less than

£149 000 was sent a form in 1988 but estimates are included for this 'cut off' sector along with estimates for non-respondents and companies not registered for VAT.

Services

Separate inquiries on the service trades were undertaken in every second year from 1979 to 1985 and, from 1986, they have been conducted annually. The survey primarily provides information for national accounts purposes, including estimates of capital expenditure. Data are regularly collected on total turnover, number of businesses and capital expenditure. There is also a rotating topic which appears in selected years and, in the 1988 survey, this topic was stocks. The results of the inquiry are published annually in *Business Monitor SDA 29 Services*.

As with the retailing and wholesaling inquiries, the survey is based on VAT records and, in the 1988 inquiry, forms were sent to a random sample of 23 000 businesses. The 1988 results are based on a response rate of 89 per cent of the total number of forms sent out.

The inquiry covers businesses in various service trades and, in recent years, coverage of these trades has been expanded. Up to 1985, only total figures for the business services sector as a whole were included but, from 1985 onwards, specific sectors have been covered and these are listed in Table 6.4. New areas covered for the first time in 1986 were private education services, opticians, private hospitals and nursing homes, legal services and scientific and research services. The 1987 inquiry also covered general medical practitioners and dentists. A list of the sectors where published information is available is given in Table 6.4.

Commodities and products

Sales statistics

Information on specific products is available from another Business Monitor series containing data on sales, imports and exports. This series was started in the 1960s and, until the middle of 1989, its 170 individual titles were published quarterly. The quarterly series was known as the Business Monitor PQ Series with individual PQ titles relating to specific sub-sectors of manufacturing. Each monitor had a four-digit sector code based on the SIC. For example, *Business Monitor PQ 4283* covered soft drinks and *Business Monitor PQ 4722* covered household and personal hygiene products of paper.

Table 6.4 Service sectors in *Business Monitor SDA 29*

Business Services
Advertising & Market Research
Industrial/Commercial Valuers, Auctioneers & Transfer Agents
Chartered or Company Secretaries (firms acting as)
Computer Services
Contract Cleaning
Management Consultants
Staff Bureaux & Employment Agencies
Duplicating, Calculating & Typewriting Agencies
Other Business Services

Professional & Scientific Services
Opticians
Accountants
Miscellaneous Private Educational Services
Legal Services
Private Hospitals
Private Nursing Homes
Research & Development Services
Surveying
Architects (private practice)
Draughtsmen (private practice)
Consultant Engineers
Research Chemists, Analytical Chemists, Assayers, Non-Medical Bacteriologists, Metallurgists & Geologists
Artists, Sculptors, Designers, Authors, Journalists (freelance) & Composers
Other Professional & Scientific Services

Road Transport & Ancillary Transport Services
Omnibus & Tramway Services
Taxis & Private Hire Cars
Road Haulage Contracting, for general hire or reward; other Road Haulage
Shipping Agents/Forwarding Agents, Travel Agents, Driving Instruction, Operation of Car Parks, Toll Roads & Toll Bridges, Other Transport Services/Storage

Table 6.4 concluded

Personal and Miscellaneous Services
Cinemas, Theatres, Music Halls etc., Radio & TV Services
Film Recording Studios etc., Performers and Performing Groups, Drama, Music, Variety etc.
Dance Halls & Dancing Schools, Sport, Other Recreation, Betting, Gaming
Launderettes, Laundries, Hire of Towels, Linen & Industrial Clothing, Dry Cleaning, Job Dyeing & Carpet Beating etc., Photography
Hairdressing & Manicure, Repair of Boots & Shoes
Funeral Direction, Cemeteries and Crematoria
Other Personal and Miscellaneous Services

Following a review of the DTI's statistical activities in 1988, it was decided that there was no government need for quarterly information on products sold and much of the detail previously collected quarterly is now only collected annually. For 41 sectors, information is still collected quarterly and published in the Business Monitor PQ Series. For the other titles, the quarterly series finished in the second quarter of 1989 and these are now published annually in the Business Monitor PAS Series. A list of all these Monitors is given in the bibliography.

Sales information for the Business Monitors is collected through statutory inquiries to a sample of UK companies in each sector. Samples are usually taken from companies above a specified employment size. Notes at the beginning of each published monitor describe the sample size used and the percentage of the sector thought to be covered by the sample.

The minimum threshold, below which companies are excluded from the sample, varies from one Business Monitor to another and can also change over time. In *Business Monitor PQ 2511 Inorganic Chemicals*, only companies with over 100 employees are included in the sample although, up to 1990, companies with over 75 employees were included. For *Business Monitor PAS 3454 Electronic Consumer Goods and Miscellaneous Equipment*, the minimum employment size of companies included in the sample is only 25 employees.

Estimates may also be made for sales from companies not required to make returns. Sales figures for the sector in total and for various individual product headings within that sector are included in each Business Monitor. The sales figures refer to sales by UK manufacturers. In the quarterly series, sales figures for specific products cover the last five quarters and the latest two full calendar years. In the annual series, sales figures are given for the last six years.

The latest statistics are often provisional figures identified by the code 'P' and these are likely to be revised, coded 'R', in subsequent issues. All the Monitors give value figures for sales in £000s and a large number also give volume figures for sales, usually either the actual numbers sold or the total weight of items sold.

The sales information is supported by statistics on imports and exports for the major product headings, using data supplied by HM Customs and Excise. Usually, only value figures are included, again in £000s, although a few Monitors have volume figures. Most Business Monitors also contain statistics of producer prices for the main products included in the Monitor and an output index for the sector. Some Monitors have employment data and a few have details of consumer spending and retail prices.

The inclusion of product sales, import and export data in one publication is useful because it means that an estimate of market size for a particular product can be obtained by calculating the following:

UK Manufacturers Sales − Exports + Imports

This estimate is usually referred to as 'apparent consumption' and is used as a measure of market size in many market surveys and trade journal features which make calculations based on official statistics.

In practice, this calculation is not always that easy because product sales figures and import/export data are based on different classifications. Sales figures are based on the SIC but trade data is based on two different classifications known as the SITC and HS classifications respectively. These are described in more detail in the next section.

Sometimes, trade data does not exist for a product identified in the sales table and vice versa. In other cases, the product heading used in the sales table may not be comparable with the heading used in the import and export tables. The SIC, SITC and HS have undergone various revisions over time so it may be difficult to find a consistent heading over a number of years.

The problem of reconciling product sales data with product import and export data should be eased with the introduction of PRODCOM, a scheme of harmonized European product sales statistics being developed by the Statistical Office of the European Community (Eurostat). Most EC countries use different product classifications for their product sales statistics but PRODCOM's harmonized statistics scheme is due for implementation in 1993 and will have the legal backing of an EC regulation.

The UK will adopt the legal requirements of the PRODCOM scheme. Although this will result in changes to many of the current product descriptions, the product data should correlate directly with trade data as the product lists are based on overseas trade headings.

The complete Business Monitor series covers over 3 000 product headings. It is the main source of product information in the UK although published information on all the headings does not appear on a regular basis for a number of reasons. First, there is the problem of confidentiality. Government statistics must not give information on the operations of specific companies and, in some product areas, it may be possible to work out a company's market share figure from the Business Monitor data. This is particularly true where one or two companies dominate a sector or one company is the sole producer in a sector. In these circumstances, although the information is collected, it will not be published.

In individual Business Monitors, information for specific product headings may be treated as confidential while information for other headings is published. A product area may be treated as confidential in one time period but statistics may be published in another issue. A number of complete Business Monitors are also never published because of confidentiality reasons and these are listed in Table 6.5.

Sometimes, the figure for a particular product heading is not published because the response rate from companies has been insufficient. Again, the response rates can vary from one time period to another. If the sales figures for a specific product are very small then this data is likely to be merged with other products in a general heading.

An ideal Business Monitor has a full page of statistics like the example in Table 6.6, but, in other cases, the above restrictions can create gaps and omissions. Table 6.7 is taken from *Business Monitor PAS 3301 Office Machinery*. This lack of data, and changes to the amount and nature of data available over time, is frustrating for the user and makes the compilation of an historical series of statistics difficult.

A further frustration comes from *Business Monitor PO 1000 Index of Commodities and Business Monitor Titles* which is an alphabetical index

Table 6.5 Business Monitors not published

Activity Heading	Title
1115	Solid fuels
1200	Coke ovens
1520	Nuclear fuel
1700	Water supply
2210	Iron & steel
2220	Steel tube
2235	Other drawing, cold rolling & forming of steel
2565	Explosives
3111	Ferrous metal foundries
4130	Preparation of milk & milk products
4160	Grain milling
4200	Sugar & sugar by-products
4214	Cocoa, chocolate & sugar confectionery
4221	Compound animal feeds
4222	Pet foods & non-compound animal feeds

of all the product headings covered by the various Business Monitors with a list of the Business Monitor titles. Next to each product heading is a reference to the relevant Business Monitor number. This index is produced automatically from the product headings on the inquiry forms sent out to businesses and, as a result, has one major drawback for users. Every product heading covered by the questionnaires is included even when published statistics are not available for the reasons noted above. In other words, the index suggests that a figure exists but, in the relevant Business Monitor, the heading might be blank.

The published index is also only updated occasionally so details of new product headings or discontinued product headings may not be included. The latest version of the index was published in 1991 updating the previous index published in 1984.

The Business Monitor series is concerned with sales by UK manufacturers so it is of little use for products with negligible or no UK production facilities. It is also unlikely to cover new sectors in any

Table 6.6 Annual sales of ceramic goods by United Kingdom manufacturers (a) PAS 2489

Units in scope of the annual sales inquiries: (a)	No of enterprises (b) 1989	Units	1984	1985	1986	1987	1988	1989
Sanitaryware:								
Of vitreous china, sold without fittings	7	£millions	113.9	114.8	117.4	133.4	163.7	172.7
		Thous	**6 879**	**6 792**	**7 127**	**7 499**	**8 071**	**7 552**
Of fireclay	5	£millions	8.6	7.3	9.7	10.2	7.4	9.0
Electrical ware of ceramic materials, including insulators and insulator fittings	14	£millions	50.5	56.3	54.6	54.3	57.3	60.9
Laboratory, industrial and agricultural ceramic ware (non-refractory) excluding electrical ware and goods of fireclay	10	£millions		10.8			10.0	
Ceramic ware components including those for use in engineering but excluding agricultural, industrial and electrical ware and goods of fireclay	–	£millions	15.7	6.3	18.4	17.5	9.0	27.0
Glazed wall, floor and fireplace tiles	7	£million	81.0	84.1	89.0	100.2	110.2	106.9
		Th sq m	**15 018**	**14 671**	**14 454**	**18 024**	**15 913**	**13 638**
Tableware, domestic and toilet ware, ornamental ware and articles of furniture:								
China or porcelain:								
Table and kitchenware	12	£millions	106.5	126.0	123.3	125.3	147.2	168.6
Other:	15	£millions	56.1	67.0	69.3	72.3	79.6	90.2
Earthenware:								
Table and kitchenware	25	£millions	143.1	158.7	172.0	180.8	192.6	213.0
Other	10	£millions	14.7	16.9	21.3	20.1	19.2	18.5
Stoneware:								
Table and kitchenware	7	£millions	9.3	9.2	15.7	8.6	11.6	14.6
Other	–	£millions	6.1	6.8		6.7	7.2	7.1
Other pottery (including jet, rockingham, samian and terra cotta):								
Table and kitchenware	3	£millions	10.2	14.0	15.6	15.7	18.5	19.8
Other	9	£millions	3.7	5.2	7.6	9.3	11.5	14.5
Kiln furniture – ceramic products for the making of pottery (stilts, pillars, bats, props, saggars, etc.)	7	£millions	13.6	13.4	14.9	15.6	16.6	17.4
Tiled hearth and fireplace surrounds	4	£millions	1.8	1.8	1.8	2.0	2.1	2.2

Source: HMSO

Table 6.7 Annual sales of electronic consumer goods and miscellaneous equipment by United Kingdom manufacturers (a) PAS 3454

Units in scope of the annual sales inquiries: (a)	No of enterprises (b) 1989	Units	1984	1985	1986	1987	1988	1989
Television broadcast receivers:								
Capable of receiving viewdata but not teletext	–	£millions	0.8	4.0		3.2	–	–
		Thous	**2**	**10**	2.0	**7**	–	–
Capable of receiving viewdata and teletext	–	£millions		1.2	**5**	–	–	–
		Thous	147.1	**3**		–	–	–
Capable of receiving teletext but not viewdata	–	£millions	**622**	140.3	150.8	235.6	–	–
		Thous		**595**	**619**	**918**	–	–
Capable of receiving viewdata and/or teletext	7	£millions	–	–	–	–	330.0	224.4
		Thous	–	–	–	–	**1,259**	**951**
Other television broadcast receivers:								
Monochrome	–	£millions	7.5	9.8	7.4	3.2	2.3	– (f)
		Thous	**205**	**251**	**171**	**81**	**54**	–
Colour:								
With tube size up to 39 cm	–	£millions	69.6	91.2	85.4	97.2	–	–
		Thous	**571**	**803**	**767**	**813**	–	–
With tube size of 40 cm and over	–	£millions	268.9	247.4	269.9	252.4	–	–
		Thous	**1 450**	**1 310**	**1 363**	**1 226**	–	–
With screen size not more than 42 cms	7	£millions	–	–	–	–	104.2	93.9
		Thous	–	–	–	–	**832**	**696**
With screen size more than 42 cms but not more than 52 cms	6	£millions	–	–	–	–	53.9	99.8
		Thous	–	–	–	–	**336**	**434**
With screen size more than 52 cms	7	£millions	–	–	–	–	116.9	127.1
		Thous	–	–	–	–	**543**	**652**
Video tape recorders and video disc players (b)	9	£millions	–	144.5	188.3	230.5	291.7	302.8
Portable radio recorders	–	£millions	0.1	–	–	–	–	–
		Thous	**6**	–	–	–	–	–
Combination radio receivers, record decks, tape decks and compact disc players (music centres)	–	£millions	51.3	42.4	43.7	(d)	(d)	– (d)
		Thous	**560**	**468**	**408**	–	–	–
Domestic radio receivers with integral loudspeakers (including radio cassette recorders)	–	£millions	–	–	–	–	1.5	1.6
		Thous	–	–	–	–	**35**	**34**

Source: HMSO

great detail if at all. It takes time for new product areas to be added because government statisticians are unlikely to cover a sector until it has become established and its structure and sales are relatively stable.

Import and export statistics

While basic data on product imports and exports are included in the above Business Monitor series, more detailed and more up-to-date information is found in the monthly publication *Business Monitor MM20 Overseas Trade Statistics of the UK*. An annual volume is also published.

Individual entries for specific products give import and export figures for the latest month, and the year-to-date, with additional data on the major importing and exporting countries. Values are given in £000s and, in most cases, a volume figure is available covering the number of units or the total weight, or both. The publication also includes a brief summary of total UK trade and trade by country.

Records of overseas trade are amongst the oldest that have been regularly collected with the first series dating back to the thirteenth century. The growth of commerce at the end of the Elizabethan era emphasized the need for accurate trade statistics and the recording of import and export details of specific commodities for tax and duty purposes has continued to the present day. The published trade statistics are a by-product of this exercise carried out by HM Customs & Excise.

Published statistics on product imports and exports are based on two classification schemes. The first is the United Nation's Standard International Trade Classification (Revision 3) usually referred to as the SITC. The basic divisions and sections of this classification are given in Table 6.8.

Individual product headings within each division have a four-digit or five-digit code. Division 88 is Photographic Apparatus, Equipment and Supplies and Optical Goods, N.E.S.: Watches and Clocks. Specific product headings in the division include 881.21 Cinematographic Cameras. In all, 3 100 commodity headings are covered by this classification and the published country breakdowns of specific product imports and exports are based on this classification. Table 6.9 shows an example for product heading 882.3.

A more detailed classification, introduced at the beginning of 1988, is the Harmonised Commodity Description and Coding System (HS).

Table 6.8 Division and section titles of the Standard International Trade Classification (Revision 3)

DIVISION	00	Live animals other than animals of Division 3
	01	Meat and meat preparations
	02	Dairy products and birds' eggs
	03	Fish (not marine mammals), crustaceans, molluscs and aquatic vertebrates and preparations thereof
	04	Cereals and cereal preparations
	05	Vegetables and fruit
	06	Sugar, sugar preparations and honey
	07	Coffee, tea, cocoa, spices, and manufacturers thereof
	08	Feeding stuff for animals (not including unmilled cereals)
	09	Miscellaneous edible products and preparations
SECTION	0	Food and live animals
DIVISION	11	Beverages
	12	Tobacco and tobacco manufactures
SECTION	1	Beverages and tobacco
DIVISION	21	Hides, skins and furskins, raw
	22	Oil seeds and oleaginous fruit
	23	Crude rubber (including synthetic and reclaimed)
	24	Cork and wood
	25	Pulp and waste paper
	26	Textile fibres (other than wool tops) and their wastes (not manufactured into yarn or fabric)
	27	Crude fertilizers other than those of Division 56 and crude minerals (excluding coal, petroleum and precious stones)
	28	Metalliferous ores and metal scrap
	29	Crude animal and vegetable materials, N.E.S.
SECTION	2	Crude materials, inedible, except fuel
DIVISION	32	Coal, coke and briquettes
	33	Petroleum, petroleum products and related materials

Table 6.8 continued

	34 Gas, natural and manufactured
	35 Electric current
SECTION	3 Mineral fuels, lubricants and related materials
DIVISION	41 Animal oils and fats
	42 Fixed vegetable fats and oils; crude, refined or fractionated
	43 Animal and vegetable oils and fats, processed, and waxes of animal or vegetable origin; inedible mixtures or preparations of animal or vegetable fats and oils, N.E.S.
SECTION	4 Animal and vegetable oils, fats and waxes
DIVISION	51 Organic chemicals
	52 Inorganic chemicals
	53 Dyeing, tanning and colouring materials
	54 Medicinal and pharmaceutical products
	55 Essential oils and resinoids and perfume materials: toilet, polishing and cleansing preparations
	56 Fertilizers (other than those of Group 272)
	57 Plastics in primary forms
	58 Plastics in non-primary forms
	59 Chemical materials and products, N.E.S.
SECTION	05 Chemicals and related products, N.E.S.
DIVISION	61 Leather, leather manufactures, N.E.S. and dressed furskins
	62 Rubber manufactures, N.E.S.
	63 Cork and wood manufactures (excluding furniture)
	64 Paper, paperboard, and articles of paper pulp, of paper or of paperboard
	65 Textile yarn, fabrics, made-up articles, N.E.S. and related products
	66 Non-metallic mineral manufactures, N.E.S.
	67 Iron and steel
	68 Non-ferrous metals
	69 Manufactures of metal, N.E.S.

Table 6.8 concluded

SECTION	6 Manufactured goods classified chiefly by material
DIVISION	71 Power generating machinery and equipment
	72 Machinery specialized for particular industries
	73 Metalworking machinery
	74 General industrial machinery and equipment, N.E.S. and machine parts, N.E.S.
	75 Office machines and automatic data processing machines
	76 Telecommunications and sound recording and reproducing apparatus and equipment
	77 Electrical machinery, apparatus and appliances, N.E.S. and electrical parts thereof (including non-electrical counterparts, N.E.S., of electrical household type equipment)
	78 Road vehicles (including air cushion vehicles)
	79 Other transport equipment
SECTION	7 Machinery and transport equipment
DIVISION	81 Prefabricated buildings; sanitary, plumbing, heating and lighting fixtures and fittings, N.E.S.
	82 Furniture and parts thereof; bedding, mattresses, supports, cushions and similar stuffed furnishings
	83 Travel goods, handbags and similar containers
	84 Articles of apparel and clothing accessories
	85 Footwear
	87 Professional, scientific and controlling instruments and apparatus, N.E.S.
	88 Photographic apparatus, equipment and supplies and optical goods, N.E.S.: watches and clocks
	89 Miscellaneous manufactured articles, N.E.S.
SECTION	8 Miscellaneous manufactured articles
SECTION	9 Commodities and transactions not classified elsewhere in the SITC

Table 6.9 Example of commodity classifications and country breakdowns for product heading 882.3

882.3 Photographic film in rolls, sensitized, unexposed (O/T of paper or fabric); instant print film in rolls

Section 8		June 1990		6 months ended June 1990	
		Qty	Value £ thous	Qty	Value £ thous
	HKG	11 866	25 461	66 273	132 476
E.C.	HKG	6 941	12 842	35 163	62 813
France	HKG	1 270	3 560	6 703	18 249
Belgium–Luxem.	HKG	1 319	1 937	7 000	9 078
Netherlands	HKG	641	962	4 190	8 358
F.R. of Germany	HKG	2 514	3 086	12 898	18 446
Italy	HKG	1 149	3 190	4 197	8 416
Japan	HKG	1 159	2 215	9 485	14 794
U.S.A.	HKG	3 495	9 808	18 805	49 778
Other countries	HKG	319	704	2 995	5 358

In the UK, this classification has a nine-digit code for specific products and over 10 000 commodity headings are included. In the published monthly statistics, this classification is used to provide total import and export data for more detailed product headings than the SITC although no country breakdown is given. Table 6.10 shows an example.

Each issue of the monthly *Overseas Trade Statistics of the UK* has an alphabetical index with details of all the relevant SITC codes but there are no indexes covering the nine-digit codes of the HS. Details of these, and their links with the SITC codes, are included in a separate publication, *Guide to the Classification of Overseas Trade Statistics*, updated annually. This guide is essential if a detailed use is to be made of the monthly trade statistics.

Other publications covering UK trade include the *Monthly Review of External Trade Statistics*, with an analysis of imports and exports by major product group; *Business Monitor MQ10 Overseas Trade Analysed in Terms of Industries*, with a quarterly analysis of commodities traded according to the industries of which they are principal products; and

Table 6.10 Example of HS classification

882.3 Photographic film in rolls, sensitized, unexposed (O/T of paper or fabric); instant print film in rolls

Section 8		June 1990		Period ended June 1990	
		Qty	Value £ thous	Qty	Value £ thous
370210000	KG	13 627	234	86 257	1 396
	SQM	28 880		331 388	
370220000	KG	10 853	65	13 543	127
	NO	2 904		19 233	
370231100	KG	3 368	114	83 199	1 213
	NO	112 470		685 068	
370231900	KG	39 115	1 904	195 004	11 870
	MTR	3 544 623		31 310 053	
370232110	KG	54 911	780	242 932	3 697
	SQM	140 897		818 080	
370232190	KG	4 476	86	38 367	683
370232310	KG	32 858	490	111 998	1 431
	SQM	97 175		311 555	
370232510	KG	123 698	1 389	811 960	9 763
	SQM	452 190		3 516 912	
370232910	KG	4 556	27	20 441	167
	NO	19 120		102 324	
370232990	KG	2 086	93	14 080	653
	MTR	232 361		3 542 903	
370239000	KG	64 214	242	433 002	2 454
	SQM	962 755		2 963 175	
370241000	KG	94 375	4 791	214 102	11 389
	SQM	503 117		1 159 298	
370242000	KG	53 662	832	372 648	5 200
	SQM	362 395		2 604 502	
370243000	KG	32 880	613	206 938	3 823
	SQM	118 092		1 817 020	
370244000	KG	103 996	1 539	519 232	8 203

Table 6.10 concluded

		Qty	Value £ thous	Qty	Value £ thous
	SQM	929 443		3 255 042	
370251100	KG	28 255	992	178 504	5 525
	NO	1 591 973		7 536 728	
370251900	KG	79	3	3 089	54
	NO	1 032		237 972	
370252100	KG	33 850	591	153 326	2 056
	NO	877 725		3 071 623	
370252900	KG	10 189	431	80 708	2 404
	MTR	1 846 308		8 746 495	
370253000	KG	6 416	252	45 229	908
	NO	154 992		634 230	
370254000	KG	204 161	4 709	985 137	23 068
	NO	5 170 650		22 518 381	
370255000	KG	149 610	3 876	1 092 733	28 345
	MTR	17 275 433		234 789 942	
370256100	KG	53	2	3	2
	NO	300		300	
370256900	KG	1 031	83	3 937	235
	MTR	131 705		540 521	
370291100	KG	36	3	387	13
	NO	270		1 700	
370291900	KG	1 320	25	1 982	35
	NO	7 177		7 595	
370292100	KG	—	—	68	2
	MTR	—		6 835	
370292900	KG	6 003	322	20 653	1 023
	MTR	372 931		1 836 023	
370293100	KG	—	—	930	27
	NO	—		3 416	
370293900	KG	4 226	94	11 004	364
	NO	61 666		240 449	
37029410	KG	2 664	48	14 199	246
	MTR	117 195		272 430	
370294900	KG	5 614	162	39 468	916
	MTR	684 090		3 643 262	
370295001	KG	210	4	9 760	82
370295009	KG	94 227	666	622 436	5 104

UK External Trade: Area Commodity Analysis, a quarterly publication showing UK trade with the key geographical areas.

More detailed trade tabulations are available from various 'marketing agents' appointed as agents by HM Customs and Excise. These private companies have access to all the import and export statistics and offer a number of services including statistics on any traded product, in the SITC or HS classification, by value, volume and country, plus additional data on the port of entry or departure, and carrier or container depot used. For example, statistics comparing one UK airport's imports of a specific product with another's can be produced on a regular basis. Data can be supplied in hard copy format, on disc or magnetic tape and on a regular or ad-hoc basis. The companies offering these services are listed below and their full addresses are given in the Appendix:

Abacus Data Services (UK) Ltd
Business & Trade Statistics Ltd
Data Star
Interactive Market Systems (UK) Ltd
Maritime & Distribution Systems (Overseas Trade Data)

Trade statistics are based on information supplied by the traders themselves who are required to put the goods into the appropriate heading of the classification.

Errors do occur and most of these are inevitably passed on to the trade statistics. The Rayner Review of government statistics noted that approximately 27 per cent of export documents contained errors. The monthly statistics are published quickly and are based on unchecked data from traders' documents. A sample of records are checked by customs officials and, where errors are discovered, the figures are revised in the annual volume.

The complexities and time lags involved in international trade can also affect the figures. UK trade figures may show that a certain amount of product A was imported into country X but country X may not actually have imported this amount. All or some of the amount may have been re-exported by country X to another country. Imports into the UK from country X may also have initially originated from another country. Different countries may use slightly different product definitions and different methods of measuring imports and exports.

With the advent of the Single Market in the European Communities, frontier controls will be abolished and the traditional method of collecting trade statistics will disappear as duties and taxes on imports and exports will no longer apply. To maintain the supply of trade statistics for intra-EC trade, it is proposed that import and export information will be collected from VAT forms sent out to a sample of companies. Detailed monthly commodity trade figures will be collected from large traders above certain thresholds and global estimates will be obtained from smaller traders. Businesses falling below the VAT threshold will be excluded. The traditional method of collecting trade statistics will be maintained for trade with countries outside the EC.

Machine readable data

Trade statistics are available on-line but Census of Production data and the product data from the Business Monitor series are not available on-line. Data on industries and products can be supplied on magnetic tape, discs or as a print-out from the Industrial Economic Indicators Database. This database, based on official statistics, is available from Business and Trade Statistics Ltd (see Appendix 1 for details).

The database was originally prepared by the Department of Trade and Industry for use by government economists and statisticians and it contains data relating to industrial activity, production, sales, prices, exports, imports, home consumption and employment. There are over 90 variables for more than 300 industries, with some series going back to 1973. The series can be quarterly, monthly or annual and the database is updated monthly.

Semi-official sources

The distinction between official and non-official sources of statistics is complicated by the fact that some organizations operate as separate units but are funded or supported in some way by central government. A number of these organizations produce important statistical series in particular sectors, and before looking at non-official sources in detail, it is worth mentioning some of the main semi-official producers.

The National Economic Development Office (NEDO) publishes regular and occasional reports on industrial trends and sectors and its

Joint Forecasting Committee for the Construction Industries produces quarterly *Construction Forecasts*.

Many of the marketing boards and authorities in food and agriculture publish annual, quarterly and monthly statistics. Examples include the Milk Marketing Board, Potato Marketing Board, the Sea Fish Industry Authority and the Home Grown Cereals Authority.

The British Tourist Authority and the individual tourist boards have an extensive range of statistical publications, including the *British Tourism Survey* and specific reports on visitors, tourist attractions, tourism expenditure, tourism forecasts and regional trends. Regular travel and trade data comes from the Civil Aviation Authority and the British Ports Authority.

Non-official sources

Like official sources, non-official statistics cover general industry trends and specific product and market information. The section below describes some general sources and this is followed by sources on specific sectors.

General sources

Industrial and business trends surveys

Opinion surveys of business executives aim to give an early indication of forthcoming changes in the industrial and business climate. They do not measure actual changes but ask business people about their expectations and the prospects for their particular business. The responses are aggregated and the aggregate result of the replies to a specific question is usually expressed as a 'balance' figure. The balance figure is the difference between the number or percentage of respondents replying positively to a question, for example, 'more', 'up' or 'more optimistic', and those replying negatively to a question, for example 'down', 'less' or 'less optimistic'.

The CBI Industrial Trends Survey is the most widely reported survey of recent and forthcoming industrial trends. The survey started in 1958 and, from 1958 to 1971, it was published three times a year. From 1972 onwards, it has been quarterly with publications at the end of January, April, July and October. Since 1975, there has also been an abbreviated *Monthly Enquiry* which uses five questions from the quarterly survey.

The survey obtains opinions from a sample of around 1 200 respondents per quarter. A general question asks 'are you more, or less optimistic than you were four months ago about the general business situation in your industry?' Other questions consider specific areas such as export prospects, capital expenditure trends, output, order books, new orders and employment. Replies are weighted according to the proportion of manufacturing net output accounted for by the firm's industry/employment size group.

The results are published within two weeks of the closing date for replies so the information is up-to-date. Because it is based on the opinions of decision makers in industry, it claims to be an early indicator of industrial changes which later appear in the official statistical series.

Published results are arranged under SIC (1980) Revised headings with 50 individual industry sections, 12 broad industrial groupings and four employment size groups. Each section gives the number of respondents in that sector and figures cover the last four months and expected trends in the next four months. Backdated data at a disaggregated level is available from the CBI.

Other business opinion surveys from the CBI are the quarterly *CBI/FT Distributive Trades Survey*, published since 1983 in association with *The Financial Times*, and the *CBI/Coopers Deloitte Survey of the Financial Services*. The distributive trades survey covers 22 individual sectors in retailing and wholesaling.

In August 1990, a new regional survey was introduced based on a sample of the respondents to the industrial trends survey. This quarterly *Regional Trends Survey* is produced in association with Business Strategies Ltd (BSL).

Another opinion survey of business trends is the *Business Expectations Survey* produced by Dun & Bradstreet. Every quarter, approximately 1 300 managing directors from a cross-section of British commerce and industry are questioned on the prospects for their companies in the coming three months. Opinions are sought on trends in sales, new orders, employment, exports, selling prices, profits and advertising expenditure.

The basic results are published in a press release where the results are also broken down by region and by broad industry sectors like durable manufacturers, non-durable manufacturers, wholesalers, retailers, services, agriculture, construction and mining. More detailed information is available from Dun & Bradstreet.

The Institute of Directors publishes a *Poll of Members' Opinions* six times a year although this is based on a smaller sample of approximately 300 business leaders.

Industrial performance data

Aggregate data on business performance is calculated from the financial results and earnings of individual companies. *Industrial Performance Analysis*, published annually by Inter Company Comparisons (ICC), measures the financial performance of 206 production, distributive and service sectors over a three-year period using 18 key financial ratios. The aggregate data is based on the financial results of over 15 000 leading UK companies.

Dun & Bradstreet's annual *The Guide to British Business Performance*, is based on an analysis of 200 000 companies with 20 ratios for 370 sectors, classified according to the US Standard Industrial Classification. Services, mining, construction and agriculture, forestry and fishing are included as well as manufacturing sectors. A separate section, 'Great Britain Ltd', is a compilation of all the companies in the database, thus presenting a picture of UK business as a whole. Again, data for the latest three years is included.

Quoted UK is published annually by the stockbrokers, Hoare Govett, and gives a guide to the performance of UK industry based on the performance of the leading companies on the Stock Market. The figures are grossed up to produce a total performance figure.

Figures on company failures and bankruptcies, generally and by sector, are published quarterly by Dun & Bradstreet and Trade Indemnity.

Industrial structure

Companies such as Dun & Bradstreet and Kompass which are mainly involved in supplying information on specific companies can also supply aggregate statistics on industrial and business sectors. For example, Dun and Bradstreet's Duns Marketing Database contains information on approximately 360 000 actively trading UK businesses and the database is continually updated. Updated information is obtained in various ways including telephone interviews, postal questionnaires and monitoring Companies House records and the press.

Aggregate statistics on the number of companies and employment sizes can be supplied broken down by local areas and specific sectors of the US Standard Industrial Classification, covering agriculture, forestry, fishing, mining, construction, manufacturing and services.

Dun & Bradstreet can also link their aggregate financial performance data to these industrial structure statistics.

Market Location is a private company supplying information on specific companies and establishments to enhance sales promotion activities and sales targeting. The basis of its services is a computer file, updated daily, of establishments in agricultural, forestry, fishing, mining, industrial and service sectors in Great Britain.

In addition to supplying data on specific establishments, it can also provide aggregate data on the number of establishments by UK SIC sector, by geographical region, by postcode area and other local breakdowns and by employment size. *Database Statistics* is a booklet with basic data on the number of establishments arranged in the above categories and more detailed information is available from the company.

Specific sectors

Trade associations

Trade associations can often provide more detailed statistics on specific sectors or product areas than official statistics but the accuracy and reliability of the data can vary considerably from one association to another. The general advantages and disadvantages of using trade association data are described in Chapter 2.

There are over 6 000 trade associations in the United Kingdom but only a small percentage of these, around 8 per cent, produce statistics on a regular basis. Table 6.11 lists 63 of the major publishers but further details of the publications available, and details of other publishers, are included in *Sources of Unofficial UK Statistics* published by Gower.

Many of the larger well-established associations operate in traditional areas reasonably well covered by official statistics, such as engineering, construction, food and drink, and textiles and clothing, but newer associations are often covering sectors poorly covered by official data. Business service sectors, such as advertising, computing services, contract cleaning and leasing, and retailing and financial services are more likely to be covered in detail by a trade association than by official statistics.

Some associations, such as the Aluminium Federation, Iron & Steel Statistics Bureau and the Building Societies Association, provide data for official publications but, in most cases, trade association data is clearly separate and is not incorporated into any official series. There

Table 6.11 Trade associations – key publishers of statistics

Advertising Association
Aluminium Federation
Apparel, Knitting & Textile Alliance
Association of British Insurers
Association of Franchised Distributors of Electronic Components (AFDEC)
Association of Manufacturers of Domestic Electrical Appliances (AMDEA)
Association for Payment Clearing Services (APACS)
Biscuit, Cake, Chocolate & Confectionery Alliance (BCCCA)
Booksellers Association of Great Britain & Ireland
Brewers Society
British Bankers Association
British Carpet Manufacturers Association
British Clothing Industry Association
British Food Manufacturing Industries Research Association (Leatherhead Food R.A.)
British Footwear Manufacturers Federation
British Frozen Food Federation
British Independent Steel Producers Association
British Paper & Board Industry Federation
British Phonographic Industry Ltd (BPI)
British Plastics Federation
British Printing Industries Federation
British Radio & Electronic Equipment Manufacturers Association (BREMA)
British Road Federation
British Soft Drinks Association
British Textile Confederation
British Toy & Hobby Manufacturers Association
British Venture Capital Association
British Videogram Association
British Woodpulp Association
Builders Merchants Federation
Building Employers Confederation
Building Services Research & Information Association (BSRIA)
Building Societies Association

Table 6.11 concluded

Chemical Industries Association
Cinema Advertising Association
Confederation of British Wool Textiles
Council of Mortgage Lenders
Dairy Trade Federation
Engineering Employers Federation
Federation of Civil Engineering Contractors
Federation of Master Builders
Fertilizer Manufacturers Association
Food & Drink Federation
Furniture Industry Research Association
Hosiery & Allied Trades Research Association (HATRA)
Institute of Grocery Distribution (IGD)
Institute of Petroleum
Machine Tool Trades Association
Metal Packaging Manufacturers Association
National Association of Pension Funds
National Council of Building Material Producers (BMP)
National House Building Council
Paintmakers Association of Great Britain
Publishers Association
Research Association for the Paper & Board, Printing & Packaging Industries (PIRA)
Scotch Whisky Association
Shoe and Allied Trades Research Association (SATRA)
Soap & Detergent Industry Association
Society of Motor Manufacturers & Traders (SMMT)
Textile Statistics Bureau
Timber Trade Federation
UK Iron & Steel Statistics Bureau
Wine & Spirit Association of Great Britain & Northern Ireland
Wool Industry Bureau of Statistics

are links between trade associations and official statisticians via regular committees and meetings but in some countries, such as France, these links are much stronger: statistics from the main French associations are used as the basis for the annual industrial production and sales figures published by central government.

Examples of trade association statistics are included in selected case studies at the end of the book and this section concentrates on describing the different types of data available from associations.

Many associations simply re-package and comment on official statistics, probably using sales data from the Business Monitor series or import/export data from HM Customs & Excise. This in itself is a useful function as it can provide informed comments on otherwise bald official data.

If the user is looking for a series of figures over a number of years then an annual publication from a trade association will probably cover these in one issue and the user can avoid wading through volumes of official publications. The Annual Report of the British Carpet Manufacturers Association, for example, has a section on the state of trade with commentary and graphs on the carpet market, sales and trade covering a five-year period. All this information comes from official sources. The Wine & Spirit Association publishes a monthly survey of wine imports based on Customs & Excise data. Regular figures on beer consumption from the Brewers Society are based on an apparent consumption figure calculated from Business Monitor statistics.

The main strength of trade association statistics is that they can provide original data not available elsewhere and give information on products and sectors not included in central government statistics. Even common products like chocolate and bicycles are not included in Business Monitor sales data but associations can fill the gap: the Biscuit, Cake, Chocolate & Confectionery Alliance publishes regular statistics on the deliveries and consumption of chocolate and sugar confectionery, with specific data by type of product; and the Bicycle Association of Great Britain has statistics on UK bicycle production. Sales of televisions are published in a Business Monitor but more detailed data on televisions with specific features, such as NICAM stereo, is available from the British Radio & Electronic Equipment Manufacturers Association (BREMA).

Most official statistics concentrate on a total sales or total production figure but, in some instances, more specific information on the characteristics of the market is required. Association sources can often help by offering different types of data, such as end-user statistics, channels of distribution data, retail sales versus other sales information, regional sales data and product price information. The British Forging Industry Association, for example, compiles statistics on deliveries of steel forgings by end-user sector while the Publishers

Table 6.12 Selected UK market survey publishers

Datamonitor
Economist Publications
ERC Statistics
Euromonitor
Harvest
Key Note
Market Assessment
Mintel
Marketing Strategies for Industries (MSI)
Projection 2000

Association publishes data on book sales by type of book, student buying and retail and institutional spending. Central government publishes general figures on new car registrations but the Society of Motor Manufacturers & Traders produces statistics by make and model.

Other associations produce forecasts or opinion surveys looking at possible future trends in their sectors. The Building Services Research & Information Association has regular forecasts covering specific product areas in its quarterly statistical bulletin and the Engineering Employers Federation publishes quarterly forecasts for the main engineering sectors alongside Business Monitor data on existing sales. Many of the associations in the construction sector have regular opinion surveys of their members, looking at anticipated workloads, output and employment over the coming months.

Market survey publishers

There are various general publishers of market survey reports in the UK and a list of the major ones is given in Table 6.12. Most of these organizations concentrate on publishing one-off reports with an up-to-date analysis of a specific market, which are outside the scope of this book, but they are worth mentioning because they often incorporate data from a selection of official and non-official statistical series. The reports, usually costing between £50 and a few hundred pounds, tend to concentrate on consumer markets and may also include summary data from original consumer research (this data is described in more detail in Chapter 8).

Table 6.13 Some publishers of specialist market surveys

Company	Subject area
Context	Computers
Corporate Intelligence Grp	Retailing
Information Research	Paints
JHA Associates	Cosmetics & toiletries
Leisure Consultants	Leisure
Mackintosh Consultants	Electronics
Profile Sports Marketing	Sports
Romtec	Computers
TMS Partnership	Clothing & textiles
Verdict Research	Retailing

Established publishers, such as Key Note, Euromonitor, Market Assessment and Mintel update their reports at regular intervals while others have developed regularly updated titles and series alongside their one-off reports. Examples include: *Euromonitor's A to Z of UK Marketing Data* published every few years and *European Marketing Data and Statistics*, published annually; Market Assessment's annuals such as *Market Forecasts, Growth Markets* and *Top 400 Markets* reviewing trends in key consumer markets; the quarterly *Consumer and Economic Trends* from Projection 2000; quarterly economic reviews and product reviews and regular consumer spending statistics included in *Retail Business* published by Economist Intelligence Unit. The Henley Centre, although largely known for its economic forecasts and not really a general publisher of market surveys, publishes the regular series *Planning Consumer Markets* and *Leisure Futures*.

There are specialist companies concentrating on specific market sectors and some examples of these are listed in Table 6.13. Regular statistical reports from these companies include the annual *Leisure Forecasts* from Leisure Consultants, *Microcomputer Annual Review* published by Romtec and the annual *Silver Book,* covering cosmetics and toiletries, from JHA Associates Ltd.

As well as purchasing published volumes, users can also access many of the reports from the general market survey publishers through on-line systems. Occasionally, a subscription to the original producing body is required but, in most instances, access comes via payment to the on-line host which, in turn, pays a fee to the market survey company. The systems give users access to the range of reports produced by specific publishers and allows them to extract particular sections and items from reports.

The Market Analysis and Information Database (MAID), produced by Maid Systems Ltd, is mounted on the host bureaux, Pergamon Financial Data Services (PFDS). The database includes reports from Euromonitor, Economist Publications, Key Note and Datamonitor. The Profile host system from *The Financial Times* has data from Datamonitor, Euromonitor, Key Note, Marketing Strategies for Industry, and Mintel. Datastar has reports from Datamonitor, Euromonitor and Key Note while Harvest has its own on-line service with reports, updated daily, covering 20 general product and service areas. Key Note publications are also available from an on-line service run directly by its parent company, ICC. The addresses of these on-line systems are given in Appendix 1.

Manufacturing companies

As well as publishing annual reports and accounts, an increasing number of companies produce regular market reports on their product areas and market sectors. This is particularly true of companies operating in fast-moving consumer goods markets, usually referred to as FMCG markets. Many of the reports are produced by food and drink companies, but there are also reports on other areas such as consumer durables, cosmetics, brown goods, DIY and lifestyle trends.

These publications are another useful source of market information, often available free from the companies concerned, although they must be used with care. Most of the reports are well presented and glossily produced but the quality of the data can vary considerably with some giving unacknowledged figures and rough market estimates while others bring together data from various sources and provide full details of the sources used. Some reports are based on original market research commissioned by the company.

Most of these reports are published for public relations purposes and are often targeted at retailers and distributors to advertise a company's products, to emphasize the importance of particular brands and to show the importance of that company and its products in that particular market. Reports from different companies are likely to disagree over market sizes and the relative importance of specific products and brands. Normally, however, these disagreements are a matter of degree and the reports can still provide useful data on areas such as market sizes, consumer preferences and habits, retailing trends, ownership levels, product advertising and new product developments.

Occasionally, the disagreements between companies can get out of hand. The headlines listed below are just two of the many which have appeared in the trade press at various times in recent years. They reflect the continuing argument between two UK lawnmower companies, Flymo and Qualcast, about the size of the UK lawnmower market and their respective market shares:

Mower Sales Soar but Makers Still Squabble (*DIY Week*, 20 April 1990)

Mower Makers Disagree over Market Trends (*DIY Week*, 16 November 1990)

Since 1983, Flymo has been publishing *Power Lawnmower Statistics*, with data on market sizes and brand shares and putting Flymo as the market leader. Qualcast has consistently disagreed with Flymo's figures, complaining about the product definitions used, and has produced its own figures with Qualcast as the market leader.

Qualcast's total market size figures are smaller than Flymo's and this is at the centre of the disagreement. Flymo has accused Qualcast of underestimating the total market size so that it can inflate its own brand share claims. In 1989, the British Lawnmower Manufacturers Federation (BLMF) started to collect and publish independent figures on the lawnmower market in an attempt to stop the arguments but the squabbles have continued. The top headline above refers to a disagreement between Flymo and Qualcast on market shares based on each company's interpretation of the BLMF figures!

The situation in the lawnmower industry is the exception rather than the rule and most company reports are worth looking at because they can provide original data often accompanied by commentary and analysis. Many cover product areas unlikely to be covered by other sources. One example is Sharwood's regular review of the Indian and Chinese food sectors with market data on specialized products such as poppadums and mango chutney.

A selection of the companies involved in publishing regular market reports is given in Table 6.14 along with the main product areas covered.

Table 6.14 UK consumer markets – some company publishers

Company	**Product Area**
Bass	Drinks
Batchelors	Food & eating
Birds Eye Walls	Frozen food, ice cream, pocket-money
Bryant & May	Matches, smokers' requisites
Bulmers	Cider
Cadbury	Confectionery
Chivers Hartley	Jams & marmalade
Cow & Gate	Baby foods
Crown Berger	Paints & lifestyles
Del Monte Foods	Canned fruit & juices
Du Pont	Cookware
Eden Vale	Chilled dairy products
Ferguson	Consumer electronics
Flymo	Lawnmowers & gardening
Fort Sterling	Paper tissues
HP Foods	Sauces & ketchup
KP Foods	Snack foods
Kraft General Foods	Coffee
Lyons Maid	Ice cream
Mates	Condoms
Nabisco	Biscuits
Nestlé	Dairy products, chocolate, drinks
Perrier	Mineral water
Polycell	DIY & home improvements
Radox	Bathroom products
Ross Young	Frozen foods
Rowntree Mackintosh	Confectionery
Sharwood	Indian & Chinese food
Showerings	Cider
Smith & Nephew	Skincare
Tilda	Rice
Trebor	Confectionery
Vitalia	Food Supplements
Whitbread	Drinks

Trade journals

Trade journals are an often underestimated source of business statistics. News items and articles in journals often reproduce statistics from other sources. Other journals have regular statistical features which reproduce Business Monitor figures, trade data, prices and earnings data, trade association data and relevant market research data. Some journals carry out their own regular statistical surveys or commission other companies to carry out a survey for them. All these cases make journals a useful starting point when approaching a new subject or market area.

7 Labour Market Statistics

Labour market statistics provide information on the characteristics of the labour force, employment and unemployment levels and trends, occupations, earnings and training. These indicators help government to develop and monitor employment and training policies and measures for the unemployed. For others, including businesses, trade unions and academic users, they offer a guide to the state of the labour market in general and in specific sectors and local areas.

Some labour force statistics are contained in general socio-economic surveys like the *General Household Survey* (GHS) and *Family Expenditure Survey* (FES), described in Chapter 4, while the ten-yearly *Population Census*, described in Chapter 3, has detailed information. Alongside these sources, there are specific labour market publications which are usually the responsibility of the Department of Employment. The monthly *Employment Gazette* brings together summary labour market statistics in one source. Major surveys are the regular *Census of Employment* and the annuals *Labour Force Survey* and *New Earnings Survey*, with data on economic activity and earnings respectively. In addition, a number of non-official sources concentrate on pay and earnings data.

Table 7.1 The Standard Occupational Classification major occupational groups

1. Managers and Administrators
2. Professional Occupations
3. Associate Professional and Technical Operatives
4. Clerical and Secretarial Occupations
5. Craft and Related Occupations
6. Personal and Protective Service Occupations
7. Sales Occupations
8. Plant and Machine Operatives
9. Other Occupations

Official statistics

The framework for many of the labour market statistics is provided by the *Standard Occupational Classification* (SOC), a classification of occupations. Before describing the individual surveys in more detail, the SOC is explained in the following section.

Standard Occupational Classification (SOC)

The SOC is a classification of occupations applicable to all paid jobs currently done by economically active persons in Great Britain. The classification is a joint initiative between the Employment Department Group and OPCS and classification development was undertaken by the Institute for Employment Research at Warwick University. The first edition of the SOC was published in 1990 and it replaces previous classifications including the Classification of Occupations and Directory of Occupational Titles (CODOT) and the 1980 version of the OPCS Classification of Occupations (CO80).

The SOC has a hierarchical structure and consists of nine major occupation groups, listed in Table 7.1, broken down further into sub-major groups and minor groups. For example, major group 2 is 'Professional Occupations' and this is broken down into sub-major groups, such as 26 'Architects, Town Planners and Surveyors' and into various minor groups, such as 261 'Town Planners'.

All the main official statistical series relating to occupations will gradually convert to the SOC in the 1990s and further details about

Table 7.2 Regularly published statistics in the *Employment Gazette* – main subject categories

Employment and workforce
Unemployment and vacancies
Redundancies
Earnings and hours
Output per head
Labour costs
Retail prices
Household spending
Industrial disputes: stoppages of work
Tourism
YTS
Regional aid

SOC are available from the Occupational Information Unit at the OPCS offices in Titchfield (see Appendix 1).

General labour market statistics

The best starting points for labour market statistics are the monthly *Employment Gazette* and the press notices produced by the Department of Employment. There are two main press notices, published monthly, titled *Labour Market Statistics: Unemployment and Unfilled Vacancies* and *Details of Employment, Unemployment, Earnings, Prices and Other Indicators*.

The *Employment Gazette* contains articles and news items plus a statistical section with tables and graphs on the labour market. Tables on over a hundred separate topics in 12 general categories are published throughout the year, on a monthly, bi-monthly, quarterly, six-monthly or annual basis. Some of the categories go beyond narrow employment areas and include retail prices, household spending and a section on tourism. This latter section includes employment data but also has data on travel, tourism income and expenditure and visitors. Table 7.2 lists the general categories included in the statistical section.

Articles and occasional supplements in the *Gazette* provide the basic, and often first, results and analysis from the labour market surveys described in more detail in the following sections. Many articles appear regularly at approximately the same time each year covering important specific areas of the labour market such as registered disabled in the public sector, industrial stoppages, trade union membership, health and safety statistics and apprentices and trainees.

The labour force

The main source of data on labour force trends and characteristics is the *Labour Force Survey* (LFS). The LFS is a source of regular information on the labour market, employment, unemployment, occupation, hours of work, methods of job search, qualifications, training and other characteristics of persons involved in the labour market. The first LFS was carried out in 1973 and, up to 1983, these surveys were biennial. Annual surveys were produced from 1984 to 1991 but, on 9 March 1990, the Secretary of State for Employment announced that the survey would become quarterly from Spring 1992.

In 1973, the survey was initiated under the terms of a Regulation derived from the Treaty of Rome. Labour Force Surveys are carried out in other member states of the European Community and the EC's Statistical Office (Eurostat) collects data from the individual member countries and publishes its own *Labour Force Survey* based on these returns. Data from the LFS in each member country provides information for the EC in areas such as the allocation of the Social Fund.

In the UK, LFS results are based on interviews with the members of 60 000 households in Great Britain and this sample of households is taken from the Postcode Address File. Participation in the survey is voluntary and the response rate in recent years has been around 81–82 per cent. The survey is carried out by OPCS on behalf of the Department of Employment and a separate survey is carried out in Northern Ireland based on a sample of approximately 4 000 households. The results of the latter survey are incorporated into the published LFS reports.

The annual reports of the LFS are usually published around two years after the year to which the survey relates. For example, the annual report of the 1987 LFS was published in 1989. The reports contain commentary and statistics. Preliminary results appear in an article in the *Employment Gazette* usually in a Spring issue in the year following the survey. The April 1990 issue, for example, had the preliminary results from the 1989 survey. Various articles in the journal throughout the year also look at particular characteristics of the labour force based on LFS results. In 1990, there were articles on foreign workers, women in the labour market, union density, characteristics of the unemployed and the labour force outlook to 2001 based on LFS results and population projections. When the new quarterly survey is fully operational, the aim is to produce the first results within 12 weeks after the end of the quarter to which they relate.

Employment

There are 3 main official sources of employment data in the UK: the *Labour Force Survey*, described above, the *Census of Employment* and short-term employment estimates published in the *Employment Gazette*. Other sources include the biennial inquiries conducted by MAFF showing employment in agriculture and quarterly inquiries carried out by the Department of the Environment covering employment in the construction sector, plus the Population Census.

Prior to 1971, estimates of the number of employees were based on counts of National Insurance cards but, from 1971 onwards, Censuses of Employment have provided detailed statistics analysed by industry and area. Annual censuses were conducted from 1971 to 1978 but, following the Rayner Review of government statistics, it was proposed that these censuses should normally be carried out triennially. It was recommended that the precise frequency should depend on the overall employment situation and prevailing circumstances with the result that recent censuses have been carried out every two years. After 1978, censuses were carried out in 1981, 1984, 1987, 1989 and 1991.

The 1981 census attempted to cover all employers but these large-scale inquiries were stopped after the Rayner Review and recent censuses have been based on samples. Sampling has reduced the number of forms sent to employers in Great Britain from around 1.2 million to less than 400 000 but in Northern Ireland all employers are still covered. In 1989 in Great Britain, the sample attempted to cover all large reporting units, mainly those with 25 or more employees, plus a sample of smaller units. The large reporting units were estimated to account for approximately 85 per cent of employees.

While most censuses will continue to be based on samples, there are plans to undertake a comprehensive census in 1993 and this will be the first since 1981. The census is a statutory inquiry conducted by post in September and the response rate is high: almost 97 per cent responded in the 1989 census.

The results cover virtually the whole economy but they do exclude an increasingly important area, the self-employed, plus certain sectors such as the armed forces, homeworkers, and employees in private domestic service. There are detailed national and regional figures plus estimates for local areas such as counties, local authority areas, travel-to-work areas and parliamentary constituencies.

The basic results are published in an article in the *Employment Gazette*, usually around 18 months after the survey has been undertaken. For example, the first results of the 1989 Census were published in April 1991. Speed of publication has improved compared to earlier censuses: the results from the 1987 and 1984 Censuses took over two years to be published.

Results by industries and regions are included in the published article but more detailed analyses of the figures are available from the Department of Employment or from the National On-line Manpower Information System (NOMIS).

NOMIS has approximately 19 billion monthly, quarterly, annual and triennial population and labour statistics and, with the appropriate software, users can receive, send and manipulate the data and generate graphs and maps on their own computers. The statistics begin in 1971 and the database is updated monthly. NOMIS has two versions of the *Census of Employment*.

A 'Public Domain' file is available generally but this does not cover all the detailed data and the output is rounded. A complete file is available to authorized users under the provisions of the Employment and Training Act 1973. NOMIS is produced by the University of Durham on behalf of the Department of Employment Training Agency in Sheffield and contact points and addresses are given in Appendix 1.

Short-term employment estimates are produced on a monthly and quarterly basis and these are used, together with the Average Earnings Index, to calculate 'income from employment' which is the major component of GDP(I) (see Chapter 5) and personal sector income. They are also used in measuring productivity and unit wage costs. These estimates, published in the *Employment Gazette*, are based on the benchmark figures obtained from the Census of Employment and additional data comes from the LFS but, in between these surveys, the estimates are based on the results from a regular survey of a panel of employers. When LFS and census data appear, it may be used to revise the short-term estimates.

It became clear during the 1980s that the panel of employers used for the monthly and quarterly estimates was not an adequate representation of existing industrial or geographical employment patterns. In an attempt to improve the reliability of the estimates, a new panel was selected from respondents to the 1989 Employment Census and the first results based on this panel appeared at the end of 1991. The move to quarterly reporting of LFS results (see page 140) will also help to reduce revisions to the estimates.

Unemployment

The most widely quoted unemployment figure is the monthly unemployment rate. This is usually expressed as a percentage, and is based on a monthly count of people claiming benefits at unemployment benefit offices (UBOs). Figures are also collected by the LFS which asks individuals whether they have a job or would like work and the steps they have taken to find work.

The methods of measuring those out of work use different definitions of the unemployed and produce slightly different results for the number of people unemployed. The monthly figures are based on the claimant counts from UBOs and are often expressed as a percentage of the corresponding mid-year estimate of the workforce. This is the sum of the claimant unemployment, employees in employment, the self-employed, HM Forces and participants in work-related government training schemes.

The measure of the unemployed in the LFS is based on a definition from the International Labour Office (ILO) and this counts people without a paid job who are available to start work in the next fortnight and have either looked for work at some time in the last four weeks or are waiting to start a job already obtained. LFS figures using the ILO definition have been available for the UK since 1984 and the definition is also used by the Organization for Economic Co-operation and Development (OECD) when comparing unemployment rates between countries.

The monthly unemployment figures, published in the *Employment Gazette*, are a by-product of the administrative system used for paying benefits and the figures are derived totally from computerized records. Their main advantage is that they are regular and published relatively quickly and cheaply. They also provide data for local areas, based on returns from local offices, which would be expensive to collect using a survey method like the LFS.

The disadvantages of the monthly figures is that they have been the subject of various redefinitions and changes throughout the 1980s, which has made it difficult to monitor trends in unemployment and made comparisons with earlier figures problematic. Some of these changes were administrative, some involved changes in benefit rules, some involved changes to statistical definitions and some were technical changes made to improve the quality of the statistics. Details of these changes are described in other sources and they are not repeated here but it is worth describing one or two of the major changes.

Up to October 1982, monthly unemployment figures were based on the numbers of unemployed registered at Job Centres but, in 1982, registration at Job Centres became voluntary so this was no longer satisfactory as a measure of unemployment. This administrative change led to the monthly figure being based on the computer count of those claiming benefit at UBOs.

A change to a computer count reduced the unemployment figure slightly because of the greater accuracy in counting but others have been taken out of the count because they are not entitled to benefit. The development of various government training schemes for the unemployed has also removed various people from the unemployment count and there have been further changes in the methods of compilation due to statistical reasons. In March 1986, for example, it was decided to delay the compilation of the unemployment figures for a further two weeks so that it took place three weeks rather than one week after the specified count date. This change was introduced to reduce the previous over-recording of people who had already ceased to be unemployed before the count date.

For most of the period up to 1986, the percentage of people unemployed was expressed as a percentage of the unemployed themselves plus employees in employment (excluding the self-employed). In 1986, the self-employed and HM Forces were added to the latter group. The addition of the self-employed was logical as their numbers were growing and the unemployed can become just as much self-employed as employees but the effect of this change was to immediately cause a drop in the unemployment figures.

Self-employment figures are difficult to measure with estimates based on the population census and the LFS. When self-employment figures are revised, with the results of new surveys, the unemployment figures must be revised as well.

The cumulative effect of all the changes relating to the compilation of the monthly unemployment figures has been to reduce the published unemployment totals. This has led to suggestions that many of the changes were made to limit the adverse political effects of high unemployment. Defenders of the changes have argued that all the changes were justified leading to improved accuracy and efficiency.

What is without doubt is that the changes have made it difficult for the user of these statistics to make meaningful comparisons between figures over time. The Department of Employment has published figures for earlier periods on the new basis and, in some cases, for later periods on the old basis. For example, recent unemployment rates, based on the definition which excludes the self-employed, have continued to be published.

Regular articles in the *Employment Gazette* compare and discuss the unemployment figures produced by the claimant count and the LFS and, with a quarterly LFS (see section on the Labour Market), quarterly unemployment figures using the ILO definition will be available for the first time to complement the monthly series.

Earnings

Short term trends in earnings are measured by a monthly index of earnings published as part of a Department of Employment press release. More detailed statistics on earnings and hours come from the *New Earnings Survey* (NES), which is published annually.

The earnings index is based on a monthly survey of a sample of employers and covers manufacturing and service sectors. The index relates to payments actually made and its behaviour can be uneven from month to month so the underlying increase in the index is also calculated to smooth out the fluctuations. The monthly press release also contains figures on output per head and earnings per unit of output, usually more commonly known as labour productivity and unit labour costs respectively.

The *New Earnings Survey* (NES) is an annual survey which began in September 1968 and, from 1970, it has been carried out in April each year. Its main purpose is to obtain regular information about the levels, distribution, and make up of earnings of employees in all major industries and occupations. It covers all types and sizes of businesses in all industries and services except the armed forces and private domestic servants.

It is a survey of the earnings and hours of a random sample of one per cent of employees who are members of pay-as-you-earn (PAYE) income tax schemes in Great Britain. A separate survey is conducted by the Department of Economic Development in Northern Ireland. Information is obtained from employers not employees and a standard set of questions is asked each year and other questions are added in particular years. In 1989, 226 000 employees were selected for the sample and there was a 94 per cent response rate but some 39 000 returned questionnaires did not contain data.

The results of the survey are classified by sex, age group, sub-region of employment, collective agreement/wages council agreement, industry and occupation and the main results are published in a six-volume annual report. The six volumes are:

Part A Streamlined and Summary Analysis; Description of the Survey
Part B Analysis by Agreement
Part C Analysis by Industry
Part D Analysis by Occupation
Part E Analysis of Earnings and Hours by Region and Country and by Age Group
Part F Distribution of Hours, Joint Distribution of Earnings and Hours, Analysis of Earnings and Hours for Part-Time Women Employees

The first volume usually appears towards the end of the year to which the survey relates and the other volumes are published by the early part of the following year.

Key results are also published in the October issue of the *Employment Gazette* with other articles in other issues on particular topics in the survey. More detailed results are available from the Department of Employment at the address given in Appendix 1.

General information on incomes is available from the annual *Survey of Personal Incomes*, published by the Inland Revenue, and looking at the distribution of incomes.

The *Labour Costs Survey* goes beyond earnings and provides data on non-wage labour costs and the overall costs of labour to employers. Up to 1984, it was carried out every three years but it is now carried out every four years with surveys in 1988 and 1992.

In 1988, the survey was conducted simultaneously in all the

member states of the EC and, apart from the results published in individual member states, Eurostat publishes results for all EC countries. Estimates of labour costs are made for the years not covered by a detailed survey. Basic results are published in an article in the *Employment Gazette* and more detailed results are available from the Department of Employment.

Other official sources

Labour Market Quarterly Report, published by the Employment Department Skills and Enterprise Network, has basic statistics on the labour market well presented in coloured graphs and tables and linked to text and commentary. The results from special surveys are included in this publication.

The different types of training initiatives introduced by the Conservative government in the 1980s and the growing debate over the role of training in the economy created the need for a new publication, *Training Statistics*, which was published for the first time in 1990. It has data on training activity, training finance, training outputs and inputs, and international comparisons.

Non-official statistics

Non-official statistics concentrate on employment data and salary surveys, often related to specific professions and sectors. General employment trends, plus trends for individual sectors and regions, are described in the quarterly *Survey of Employment Prospects* published by Manpower.

This survey began in 1969 and it gives short-term forecasts, over the next quarter, of employment in specific sectors including manufacturing, services and the public sector. It is based on telephone interviews with approximately 1 500 senior executives representing the largest employers in particular categories.

The *Review of the Economy and Employment* is published approximately every 18 months by the Institute for Employment Research at the University of Warwick. It includes historical and current trends and forecasts of employment by major industry group, occupation and region. A commentary provides information on the structure of employment plus a review of recent economic developments in the economic outlook.

Specific employment and salary surveys are produced by a number of professional organizations, usually based on surveys of their individual members. Regular surveys cover professionals such as architects, bankers, lawyers, accountants, engineers and marketing and sales staff while other surveys look at other areas such as computer staff and office and clerical staff.

Examples of professional bodies involved in regular surveys are the Institute of Practitioners in Advertising (IPA), the Royal Institute of British Architects (RIBA), the Institute of Administrative Management, the Bar Association for Commerce, Finance and Industry and various engineering institutions with members from chemical engineering, civil engineering, electrical engineering and mechanical engineering. Some of the training boards, such as the Engineering Industry Training Board, produce regular reports on employment trends.

Independent companies specializing in salary surveys include Remuneration Economics, Hay Management Consultants and the Reward Group. Amongst the regular surveys of Remuneration Economics are surveys of management, engineers, financial personnel and personnel staff while a subsidiary company, Computer Economics, publishes surveys of the computer industry. The surveys from Hay Management Consultants include coverage of directors, management, office staff, financial personnel, computer staff, retail buyers and store managers. There are also regional surveys and London surveys. The *Top Jobs Rewards Survey* is published by Remuneration Economics in association with the CBI.

The Reward Group publishes surveys on specific sectors and occupations plus local salary and wage reports in 21 areas and special reports on employee benefits and performance rewards. Industry-specific reports cover construction, distribution, electronics and software, oilfields, retailing and local authorities. General surveys describe pay trends for management, directors, sales and marketing staff, clerical and operative staff, consulting engineers, research and development staff, purchasing and supply, personnel, and financial and accounting staff. Some of the latter surveys are published in association with relevant professional bodies such as the Institute of Purchasing and Supply and the Institute of Marketing.

Individual pay settlements are monitored by Incomes Data Services (IDS) and Industrial Relations Services (IRS) and the details are included in regular monthly publications. Both companies produce numerous other publications on pay, employment legislation, and labour market trends and characteristics. The latter company publishes monthly figures of average manufacturing pay settlement levels, expressed as the percentage change in settlements, in its *Pay and Benefits Bulletin*. Similar figures are produced by the CBI and the Labour Research Department (LRD). The LRD has monthly statistics for the private and public sectors, giving the percentage change in the three months up to the current month, in its monthly *Bargaining Report*. The September issue each year has a special feature on the year's trends in pay, hours and holidays.

The CBI's Pay Databank provides detailed information on pay trends in various sectors to the organizations participating in regular pay surveys. Aggregate data from the databank is published in the journal *Employment Affairs* which appears six times a year.

The deficiencies in pay data sources stem from the fact that, in most surveys, only major settlements are included and differences between local labour markets are not covered. It would be impracticable to cover every salary, wage and employment survey here but two useful sources of information are the *Directory of Salary Surveys* published annually by the Top Pay Unit of the IDS and the *National Salary Surveys – User Guide* produced by Remuneration Economics.

8 Market Research Data, Advertising and Media Information

All the statistical sources mentioned in the book so far are potential sources of market research data but this chapter concentrates specifically on those organizations providing original market research data for clients. It also has information on general sources of advertising and media data.

Most of the sources mentioned in earlier chapters of the book are available relatively cheaply but original market research data is expensive, reflecting the resources involved in setting up a survey and the collection and analysis of detailed data. The final results are unlikely to be published in traditional statistical publications and will not be available through the general library and information networks. Some basic data from original market research sources are published in general marketing data manuals and in the trade press. Examples of these sources are given in the final section of this chapter.

Selected sources of market research data have already been mentioned in other chapters and the reader is referred to the sections on socio-demographic services and opinion polls in Chapter 4 and the section on market survey organizations in Chapter 6.

Market research

Original market research is usually known as primary research or field research and involves researchers going out into 'the field' and collecting data by direct questioning. This research can be investigating industrial markets, sometimes referred to as business to business research, or consumer markets.

Research into consumer markets is more common and, apart from being of interest to consumer goods manufacturers, suppliers and retailers, it is also of major interest to advertising agencies and media organizations. Agencies need relevant market data to target their advertising at the right consumers, at the right time, in the right way and through the appropriate medium. Media organizations, like publishers, television, radio, cinemas, posters and direct mail organizations, need advertising income and thus need to be aware of the market forces affecting advertising decisions.

Most of the sources in this chapter cover consumer markets and many have been initiated or sponsored by the advertising and media sectors.

Primary research can be split into two types. First, there is ad-hoc research which is carried out on an irregular basis and is usually commissioned by a specific organization. The results are the specific interest of the commissioning organization and are normally confidential to that organization.

The second type is syndicated research or continuous research, usually initiated by a market research company, and not carried out for a particular client. The research results are sold to various clients who share the costs of the research.

Some syndicated research surveys are 'one-off' studies but, more typically, syndicated surveys are undertaken on a continuous basis with clients paying a subscription fee. It is these regular surveys which will be described in this chapter.

Research can also be quantitative or qualitative. Quantitative research usually needs a relatively large sample with the results expressed in numbers. Qualitative research can use relatively small samples and the aim is to obtain insights into respondents' attitudes, perceptions, motivations and opinions rather than generate bald figures. Group discussions and in-depth interviews are commonly used in qualitative research. Interviews and discussions are usually unstructured and, as respondents start to express views, the interviewer will encourage further elaboration of these views.

Most of the surveys mentioned here are based mainly on quantitative research.

Syndicated surveys

There are various forms of regular syndicated surveys. Some selected types are described in the following section:

Omnibus surveys

Each client pays for a small number of individual, confidential questions to be included in a regular survey. The total survey is made up of questions from various clients and questions can be added as the survey continues. The frequency of surveys can be anything from weekly to annually. Usually, a certain number of respondents are surveyed at each survey time although a fixed panel of respondents is not normally used. Questions can be asked through postal questionnaires or telephone interviews.

Consumer panels and consumer surveys

Consumer panels are fixed groups of consumers in particular market areas selected to be a representative sample of consumers in that area. Panels are mainly used to measure the purchase and consumption of products, services and brands. Data can be collected from diaries kept by individual panel members or researchers can visit specific households to check on purchases and consumption.

Consumer surveys encompass a range of surveys used to investigate the expenditure, consumption and shopping patterns of consumers along with their attitudes and opinions.

Retail audits

A regular check on purchases, stocks, prices and sales in specific retail outlets used by retailers, manufacturers and suppliers is supplied by the retail audit. The auditors visit a representative group of shops in a particular sector and the shops give the auditors permission to check such things as invoices and delivery notes. A continuous record of what is being delivered to shops, what is in stock and what is being bought is produced.

Individual shop audits usually remain the confidential property of a particular shop but aggregate data can also be produced. Audit data provide useful information on areas such as brand shares, general sales and sales by area, and average selling prices.

Additional studies can provide data on the position of particular brands, shelf space allocated to specific brands, new promotions and the effectiveness of specific outlets at selling particular products. The spread of EPOS (electronic point of sale equipment) in retail outlets has helped retail audits as computerized records of sales make data collection and analysis easier.

Readership surveys and audience surveys

Readership surveys regularly look at how many people read a specific title, as opposed to how many people buy it. Audience surveys are carried out to measure audiences for TV, radio and cinema. Both types of survey provide useful information used largely by the advertising industry and most provide additional information on the socio-economic background and attitudes of readers and viewers. There are specific surveys which examine the readership and audience patterns of particular occupations and professions but the major general surveys concentrate on trends in a particular medium, such as television, radio or newspapers and magazines.

The Institute of Practitioners in Advertising (IPA) has been particularly active in promoting readership and audience surveys with its involvement in the setting up and running of a number of Joint Industry Committees in areas of the media, such as newspapers and magazines, television, radio, cinema and posters. These joint industry committees consist of representatives from the relevant media sector, advertising agencies and advertisers and they have developed and supervised standard measures of readership and audiences.

Some of these committees have come and gone to be replaced by other bodies. A list of the major joint industry committees is given in Table 8.1 and the surveys themselves are described in a later section of this chapter.

Most of these surveys are contracted out to one or more research agencies with the contracts coming up for renewal every few years.

Market research data

There are numerous market research agencies around the country, some offering general services and others specializing in particular subject areas or services. *The Market Research Society Yearbook* lists over 250 agencies, mainly operating in consumer markets, and *The European Guide to Industrial Marketing Consultancy*, published every few years by the Industrial Marketing Research Association, lists over 70 UK consultants. It would be impracticable to decribe all these agencies here.

Table 8.1 Joint Industry Committees

JICNARS	Joint Industry Committee for National Readership Surveys
JICRAR	Joint Industry Committee for Radio Audience Research
JICREG	Joint Industry Committee for Regional Press Readership Research
JICPAS	Joint Industry Committee for Poster Audience Research, wound up in 1989 and replaced by:
OSCAR	Outdoor Site Classification and Audience Research
JICTAR	Joint Industry Committee for Television Audience Research, wound up in 1981 and replaced by:
BARB	Broadcasters Audience Research Board

The largest organizations in the consumer sector, in terms of turnover, are AGB (Audits of Great Britain) and Nielsen. Other large agencies are MAI, which includes NOP and MIL Research; Millward Brown; Research International; Taylor Nelson; and the MRB Group, including the British Market Research Bureau (BMRB).

Every year, the Association of Market Survey Organizations (AMSO) publishes a review of trends in the industry, based on figures from its 23 member companies representing the largest companies in the sector. The top companies, by turnover, are listed in Table 8.2, and some examples of the services offered by the top two companies are described below.

AGB offers a number of continuous surveys of consumer spending and purchases of goods and services through various consumer panel surveys. A subsidiary company, Attwood Statistics Ltd, runs the Attwood Consumer Panel, one of the longest established consumer panels. Other services include a regular prices audit of specific products in grocery outlets and a Television Consumer Audit (TCA), commissioned by the TV companies, providing regular reports on the

Table 8.2 Market research agencies by turnover 1990

Agency	Turnover £m
AGB	48.0
Nielsen	35.3
MAI	33.7
Millward Brown	20.3
Research International	19.0
Taylor Nelson	18.8
MRB Group	17.4
Research Business Group	9.4
Research Services Ltd	9.2
MORI	8.7
Harris Research Centre	6.6
MBL Group	5.5
Social Surveys (Gallup Poll)	5.3
Burke Marketing Research Group	4.3
Gordon Simmons Research Group	4.0
FDS Market Research Group	3.6
Public Attitude Surveys (PAS)	3.5
Martin Hamblin Research	3.4
Research & Auditing Services	2.5
Independent Research Bureau	2.0
Pegram Walters Associates	1.8
CRAM International	1.5
Scantel	1.0

Source: *AMSO Statistics 1991*

consumption of products and market trends nationally and in specific TV areas. Lek-Trak is an established retail audit in the electrical appliances sector and DIY-Trak was established in 1991 to offer a similar service for DIY retailers.

Nielsen, or A C Nielsen Company as it is more formally known, is the UK branch of the world's largest market research organization. Major activities are retail surveys and audits through the Nielsen Retail Index, which operates in various countries. The Nielsen Index Service provides a continuous measurement of retail sales and factors affecting sales for a range of product groups, including food, pharmaceuticals and confectionery. Specialist services cover wholesaling, cash and carry, and confectioners, tobacconists and newsagents. Homescan is a national household consumer panel.

The company also publishes summary data from many of the above surveys in annual reviews and titles including *Cash and Carry Trade Report, CTN Trade Report, Food Trade Report* and *Pharmacy and Drug Store Trade Report*. The annual *Nielsen Market Information Manual* has data on the value of over 250 markets with geographical and store type breakdowns.

Apart from specific services like those described above, some national surveys are undertaken by research agencies usually on behalf of industry-wide groups and organizations. Most of these surveys are commonly known by their initials and include the TGI, BARB, JICNARS, and the BMRC survey. Survey results are available from the producing organizations themselves. A number of computer service companies also offer facilities to access the data, usually providing the producing organization has given its permission. These computer companies include Interactive Market Systems (IMS), Donovan Data Services, Telmar, Holborn Research Services and United Information Services. Further details of these companies are given in Appendix 1 and the major services are described in the following paragraphs.

Target Group Index (TGI)

The TGI is produced by the British Market Research Bureau (BMRB) and is published in a series of 34 annual reports supplemented by semi-annual reports. The TGI links reading, viewing and listening to the consumption of approximately 3 000 brands in over 200 fast-moving consumer product areas and over 450 brands in other fields such as financial services, travel and airlines, cars, grocery and other retail outlets. It also produces lifestyle information based on attitude statements obtained in the survey. The data is collected through postal questionnaires to a representative sample of 24 000 adults.

In 1987, the AB TGI was introduced. This service gives a higher degree of detail than the general TGI within those areas of product purchasing and lifestyle especially relevant to heads of households/housewives in high socio-demographic status households, that is, AB households. The sample used to collect the data is an entirely separate one from that used in the broader TGI survey.

On-line access is available via BMRB or through a number of

computer bureaux. Companies offering access include IMS, Telmar and Holborn Research Services.

BARB Audience Surveys

The Broadcasters Audience Research Board (BARB) monitors television viewing habits through BARB Audience Surveys undertaken by AGB. In 1981, this joint body was established by mutual agreement of both the BBC and the ITCA with a remit to commission and supervise television audience research. Throughout the 1980s, it provided data on audiences for BBC and terrestrial commercial channels but, in the 1990s, it has been expanded to include satellite and cable television.

From August 1991, the BARB survey has been based on a sample of 4 400 households effectively increasing the sample by nearly 50 per cent from the previous size of around 3 000 households. The total sample is made up of individual area samples of between 100 and 350 households. The balance of the BARB sample is regularly monitored by Establishment Survey reports but, despite this regular monitoring, the size and composition of the sample has been the subject of criticism from the advertising profession. The changes in August 1991 have increased the sample size and they have also affected the composition of the national panel. The composition of the latest panel will be biased towards ABC1s.

An electronic meter is fitted to the television set in each household and this is capable of measuring the status of the on/off TV switch and channel selector button at one minute intervals. It can also detect the difference between video recording and actual viewing. The data provided by the meters is supplemented by viewing diaries kept by household members. Additional information is available on people present in the room when particular programmes are on, guest viewing and perceived programme quality.

The basic output of BARB is a weekly audience report, and a general press release, published a few days after the end of the week. This shows the weight of viewing of all television programmes by quarter hours throughout the day by region. It is expressed as a TVR (television rating) which is simply a percentage of those capable of receiving the programme and who were watching. Also listed are all commercials transmitted during the day. A weekly schedule of commercials is also published along with other regular reports on audience composition giving detailed demographic data. Other types of analysis are also available on request. Computer bureaux offering BARB data packages are Donovan Data Systems, IMS and Telmar.

Despite BARB's technical advances, the amount of BARB information generally available has actually been reduced since the new sample was introduced in August 1991.

There are also arguments surrounding the video viewing results. Should these be counted as part of the official ratings and included in airtime negotiations or should they be excluded?

General details of the problems associated with the new system are given in an article by Peter Fiddick in the *Guardian* (Fiddick, 1990). Fiddick states that 'it will become impossible for anyone outside a small circle of television and advertising professionals to form even the simplest picture of how, on a particular evening, British viewers apportion their time. The upshot will arguably be the least useful set of publicly available data since television audience research began'.

JICNARS

JICNARS is the Joint Industry Committee for National Readership Surveys and it is made up of representatives from publishers, advertising agencies and advertisers. It runs the National Readership Survey (NRS) which measures the readership of newspapers and magazines with breakdowns by demographic characteristics, occupation, income, households, regions and other variables. The Committee was set up in 1968 to provide a common measure of readership applicable across a range of titles and it took over the existing NRS set up by the Institute of Practitioners in Advertising in 1954.

The NRS is conducted by Research Services Ltd and it is based on a sample of approximately 28 000 adults aged 15 and over. The readership patterns of over 300 newspapers and magazines are monitored by asking a simple question: have you read or looked at this magazine/newspaper at any time in the last year for at least a couple of minutes? Respondents are shown a card with a specific title on it and if the answer is yes, further questions are asked to discover the frequency of readership and related points.

The main reports of the NRS are published at six-monthly intervals with figures covering the preceding 12 months. *NRS Bulletins* also give basic figures in advance of the main reports, early monthly estimates for newspapers and major new publications and background information on the surveys. Additional analysis and special packages are available from JICNARS and various computer bureaux, including Donovan Data Systems, IMS and Telmar. An annual report, *30 Year Readership Patterns*, published by Guy Consterdine Associates, provides historical readership data for 207 publications.

In the late 1980s, JICNARS faced heavy criticism for its failure to respond to changes in the publishing industry. It provided basic data on readership patterns but users wanted more data on specific areas such as which sections of a particular title were read, a breakdown between casual and regular readers, and the source of purchase. Further criticisms were levelled at its slow reporting and its attempt to cover too many titles. The organization of JICNARS with its maze of committees, including a main committee, a technical sub-committee and various other committees and sub-groups working on particular areas, also came under fire.

A number of companies began to look to other sources for their readership information but JICNARS responded to the criticism by an investigation into user needs culminating in proposals for a number of major changes in 1991. The committee structure was simplified by the disbanding of the technical committee and its working parties and detailed changes to the survey included faster reporting and more frequent reporting. Traditionally, early monthly estimates have been available seven to nine weeks after the fieldwork period but, from the end of 1990, they have been available within four weeks of the end of fieldwork.

Other changes included a series of questions on subject sections and topics of interest within titles, an additional question on Saturday readership of daily newspapers, quality of reading measures and a reduction in the number of titles covered. A question on the source of copy was also added in 1991.

JICRAR

The Joint Industry Committee for Radio Audience Research (JICRAR) was established in 1974 and is the newest of the individual joint-industry organizations. It measures listening patterns for independent radio, BBC radio and other selected stations in 15-minute segments over a seven-day period. The results cover individual station penetrations, hours spent listening and an individual station's share of the audience.

The survey is carried out by Research Surveys of Great Britain and is based on a sample of 20 000 adults plus a supplementary sample of children aged between 5 and 14. Respondents keep a diary record of their listening choice and the various results are published in separate quarterly, half-yearly and annual reports. Special analysis of the data is also available.

JICREG

JICREG is the Joint Industry Committee for Regional Press Readership Research. It provides circulation and readership figures for regional newspapers broken down by postcode area. JICREG took over the research programme of the Regional Newspaper Advertising Bureau (RNAB) which was disbanded in 1990.

OSCAR

OSCAR stands for Outdoor Site Classification and Audience Research and it began in 1989, taking over from JICPARS, the Joint Industry Committee for Poster Audience Surveys. It measures audiences for poster advertisements by calculating net 'opportunities to see' or 'OTS'. This is a measure of the number of chances an average member of the target audience will have of being exposed to an advert. The results are available on-line to advertising agencies and through periodic reports.

CAVIAR

CAVIAR stands for Cinema and Video Industry Audience Research and it is a regular survey of cinema-going habits and films seen, both in the cinema and on video. The survey is the responsibility of the Cinema Advertising Association (CAA) but the survey itself is carried out by a market research agency. A national sample survey of approximately 3 000 people forms the basis of CAVIAR.

The survey is sponsored by companies within the cinema and video sectors and the detailed results are only available to these companies and other subscribers to the service. Monthly cinema admission figures are also produced by the CAA with the results published in a press release and reproduced in relevant trade journals such as *Screen International*.

BMRC Businessman Survey

The business community is growing in importance as an advertising target audience and the Business Media Research Committee (BMRC) commissions a biennial survey of the reading behaviour, job status, areas of responsibility, purchasing decisions and personal characteristics of businessmen and women. The readership survey includes the national press and management publications plus trade publications specific to a particular industry or sector. The latest survey in 1990, undertaken by Research Services Ltd, asked about 150 newspapers and magazines and also looked at business people's exposure to other media, including radio and television.

The survey concentrates on business people 'of middle or higher management status whose occupation implies the exercise of significant business responsibilities'. According to BMRC, 1.15 million business people qualified in 1990 under this survey definition compared to only 832 000 in 1988. This large rise in the business population is explained by a real-life increase in the number of qualifiers, changes in the procedures for identifying business people and changes in the definition. For example, in 1990, a new definition of business people included, for the first time, younger business people in smaller companies.

Only a relatively small sample of all qualifying business people are actually used in the survey: a representative sample of 2 300 respondents was used in the 1990 survey. Interviews are conducted in the individual's home between March and August in the year of the survey and the results are published in an annual report titled *The 1990 Businessman Survey*. On-line access to the data is also available via all the computer services listed at the beginning of this chapter plus the British Market Research Bureau (BMRB) and Research Services Ltd.

Advertising expenditure

Regular advertising expenditure statistics for specific brands, products and services broken down by media type are published by two companies, Media Expenditure Analysis Ltd (MEAL) and the Media Register. The major source of broader advertising statistics is the Advertising Association.

As this book went to press, it was announced that Pergamon Market Research, the owners of the Media Register, had purchased MEAL with the likely outcome being the merging of the two services in the future. A study on how best to merge the two activities has been initiated but, in the meantime, this book treats them as two separate competing services.

Media Expenditure Analysis Ltd (MEAL) provides regular statistics on advertising expenditure by monitoring display advertisements in the national press, magazines, television and selected radio contractors. The magazines are primarily consumer-orientated publications with circulations of over 50 000 copies. It also includes national advertising in regional newspapers. Classified advertising is not covered.

Its basic quarterly publication, *Tri-Media Digest of Brands and Advertisers*, was established in 1968 and it covers 373 product groups classified into 22 broad categories. MEAL claims to cover advertisements which have appeared for over 18 000 brands. An example of the breakdown in a specific product category, Group K Household Equipment, is shown in Table 8.3. For each product group within the category, total quarterly expenditure data, plus monthly data for the latest three months and a moving annual total are included for each brand and the product group as a whole. The moving annual total is broken down by television, radio and press and the name of the agency responsible for a particular brand is also given. An example covering cookers and dishwashers, is shown in Table 8.4.

MEAL produces a number of brand expenditure reports, and most are available monthly, with titles on brand expenditure by medium, by media groups, by television regions, by area, and on radio. A monthly advertisement analysis service gives a record of each television and press advertisement placed during the latest period.

Ad-hoc requests for information can be dealt with within 24 hours and MEAL has its own on-line service split into five separate databases. MEAL data is also accessible via Donovan Data Systems, IMS, the MAID database on Pergamon Financial Data Services and the FT's Profile service (see Chapter 6 for further details), and Reuters Textline. Different services have different levels of detail and historical data. IMS and Pergamon, for example, have data from 1979 onwards, Profile from 1985 and Donovan for the latest 5 years.

The *Media Register* is a relatively recent entrant in the market with the first monthly issue in January 1986. The advertisements monitored appear in the national press, magazines and TV but there is no radio coverage. Cinema and poster advertising were added in 1991. The press coverage, however, is wider than MEAL as it includes more specialist publications and trade journals. Over 500 magazine and journal titles are included. The advertisements covered include both display and classified.

The monthly publication is arranged in 34 broad category headings and further broken down into 490 product headings. An example of a typical category heading with its product groupings is given in Table 8.3.

In each issue, the latest monthly expenditure, broken down by press and TV, is given for each brand and for the product group as a whole. Total expenditure in the previous two months and a moving

Table 8.3 Product category breakdown

MEAL

K	**HOUSEHOLD EQUIPMENT**
K01	Antiques and art galleries
K03	Baby carriages and nursery equipment
K06	Baths and sanitary ware
K09	Blankets, bedcovers, household linen
K12	Brushes and mops
K15	Carpets, rugs and underlays
K18	Castors
K21	Ceramic and plastic tiles
K24	Crockery, glass and ovenware
K27	Curtain rail and tape
K30	Cutlery and tableware
K32	Decorative laminates and plastics
K33	Domestic rubber products
K39	Fireplaces
K42	Flooring and ceiling tiles
K45	Fountain pens, ball pens and propelling pencils
K48	Furnishing and upholstery fabrics
K51	Furniture and fittings
K53	Insulation
K54	Jewellery, jewellers and silversmiths
K57	Kitchen utensils
K60	Luggage, leather goods and umbrellas
K63	Mattresses, pillows and beds
K69	Plastic houseware
K70	Safety and security devices
K71	Scales (bathroom and kitchen)
K72	Venetian and roller blinds
K75	Watches and clocks
K76	Water softeners
K78	Windows, frames, and double glazing

Table 8.3 concluded

Media Register

HFU10	Furnishings – range
HFU15	Furnishings – bathrooms
HFU20	Furnishings – bedrooms
HFU25	Furnishings – kitchen
HFU30	Furnishings – lounge
HFU35	Saunas and sunbeds
HFU40	Carpets and floor coverings
HFU45	Tiles
HFU50	Curtains and curtain rails
HFU60	Fireplaces
HFU65	Furniture upholstery and fabric
HFU67	Insulation
HFU70	Beds and mattresses
HFU72	Pillows
HFU75	Quilts and blankets
HFU77	Household linen
HFU80	Household security
HFU82	Venetian and roller blinds
HFU83	Lighting
HFU85	Double and secondary glazing
HFU90	Conservatories and home extensions

annual total, broken down by press and TV, is included. Next to each brand is the name of the agency responsible for that brand. An example covering clocks and watches is shown in Table 8.5.

While MEAL and the Media Register are the major sources of advertising expenditure data, neither can claim to have a comprehensive coverage or be totally accurate given the nature of the advertising sector. Each service excludes certain types of media from its coverage and MEAL excludes classified advertising.

Within the newspaper and magazine sectors, there are gaps in coverage in both services. MEAL base their figures on rate card costs, which are the list of charges made to advertisers published by individual publishers, television and radio companies. Rate cards are normally regarded as the starting point for negotiations rather than a set price and media owners are often prepared to negotiate rates below those of the published rate card.

Table 8.4 MEAL statistics

Household Appliances		**September 1990**							
		Qtr					**MAT**		
Product Description	**Agency**	**Total £000**	**Jul £000**	**Aug £000**	**Sep £000**	**MAT £000**	**TV %**	**Rad %**	**Prs %**
						Cookers (Gas and Electric)			
Aga cooker multifuel	Cogent	62	3	17	42	217	–	–	100
Belling cooker range – E	JWT London	225	–	–	225	225	–	–	100
Brother comb micro – E	Media Sol/Bowden	17	–	–	17	312	–	–	100
British Gas cooker	O & M Limited	1 343	43	288	1 011	6 507	85	1	14
Creda cooker range – E	Publicis Limited*	38	38	–	–	436	–	3	97
Electricity Council cookers	BSB Dorland/Zenith	164	30	1	133	2 852	63	–	37
Flavel Leisure cooker – G	Cogent	–	–	–	–	116	–	–	100
Goldstar Microwave – E	T B W A/Holmes Kngt*	–	–	–	–	307	–	–	100
Hitachi Microwave – E	Newton & Godin	–	–	–	–	341	–	–	100
Hotpoint Cooker – G&E	CIA Billett/FCA Mvty	55	–	–	55	170	–	–	100
NEFF Circotherm – E	KHBB/Zenith	92	20	29	42	480	–	–	100
Panasonic Dim 4 – E	TMD/Delaney	–	–	–	–	206	–	–	100
Panasonic Microwave – E	TMD/Delaney	–	–	–	–	556	100	–	–
Rayburn Nouvelle – M	Cogent	81	–	15	65	272	–	–	100
Sharp micro oven – E	Graham Poulter Ptnr	–	–	–	–	184	–	–	100
Sharp comb micro – E	Graham Poulter Ptnr	–	–	–	–	385	–	–	100
Toshiba microwave – E	Gold Greenlees Trott	–	–	–	–	323	–	–	100
Tefal toast & grill	Abbot MD VK SMS	–	–	–	–	173	100	–	–
Tricity cooker rge – E	Roose & Partners	201	–	–	201	201	–	–	100
Emgas cooker	Grey Network Leics	23	7	9	7	136	13	–	87

Table 8.4 concluded

Manweb cooker	Brunning Agency	10	–	–	10	86	82	–	18
N Tham Gas cooker	McCann Erickson*	–	–	–	–	68	–	–	100
N West Gas cooker	McCann Erickson Manc	151	59	14	78	591	86	–	14
Negas cooker	J W T Manchester	45	14	14	17	186	–	–	100
Norgas cooker	Robson Brown	43	13	–	30	262	82	–	18
Norweb cooker	Stowe Bowden Wilson	27	1	3	23	126	56	–	44
Scot Power cooker	Martin Tait Agency	2	–	–	2	102	87	–	13
S West Gas cooker	McCann Erickson Brst	57	–	5	51	138	58	11	31
Scot Gas cooker	Baillie Marshall Ltd	9	–	–	9	182	35	–	65
Selse cooker	KHBB/Zenith	45	16	–	28	266	–	–	100
South Gas cooker	D M B & B	48	6	5	36	165	64	–	36
W Mid Gas cooker	R T A Advertising	36	10	13	13	231	–	–	100
Other brands (56)		129	8	24	97	904	7	2	91
Total cookers (gas and electric)		2 901	269	438	2 194	17 707	53	–	47
									Dishwashers
A E G dishwasher	Young & Rubicam	114	21	–	93	345	–	–	100
Elect Cncl dishwasher	BSB Dorland/Zenith	123	32	37	55	2 479	70	–	30
Hotpoint dishwasher	CIA Billett/FCA Mvty	33	–	–	33	147	–	–	100
Miele dishwasher	TMD/Davis Wilkins	7	6	1	–	221	–	–	100
Siemens dishwasher	M C A/Wood Burden	–	–	–	–	117	–	–	100
Zanussi dishwasher	Geers Gross Adv	242	24	188	30	337	72	–	28
Norweb dishwasher	Stowe Bowden Wilson	6	–	–	6	152	82	–	18
Scot Power dishwasher	Martin Tait Agency	–	–	–	–	64	89	–	11
Other brands (16)		61	–	–	60	312	13	5	82
Total dishwashers		586	84	226	277	4 174	53	–	47

Table 8.5 Media Register statistics

February 1989

Luxury Goods (Lux)

Brand	Agency	£000	Dec	Jan	February			Moving Annual Total		
			Total	Total	Press	TV	Total	Press	TV	Total
Antiques/Auctions										
Bonhams Auction	Anderson Advert. (BE/M B S)		2.0	8.1	10.4	–	10.4	122.7	–	122.7
Christies Auctioneer	Asta Ltd		81.5	52.9	83.6	–	83.6	887.2	–	887.2
Coys Auctioneers			8.8	7.2	9.6	–	9.6	84.3	–	84.3
Great Bampton House Antiques	Handled directly		13.1	10.0	12.2	–	12.2	138.0	–	138.0
Halcyon Days Store			19.4	–	–	–	–	52.7	–	52.7
Mallett & Son (Antiques)	Handled directly		10.6	7.3	9.7	–	9.7	86.3	–	86.3
Phillips Auctioneers	Brooks Legon Bloomfi/ C.I.A.		12.7	24.2	40.2	–	40.2	588.8	–	588.8
Sothebys Auctioneers	The Russell Partnership		7.0	21.9	39.2	–	39.2	546.7	–	546.7
Spink Antiquities	Leberl		7.2	3.7	1.8	–	1.8	90.3	–	90.3
** Antiques Misc **			126.1	51.9	62.1	–	62.1	1 237.6	1.1	1 238.8
** Auctions Misc **			18.3	29.5	15.6	9.3	24.9	484.9	56.3	541.1
Sub-threshold Brands 19			25.9	7.0	8.4	–	8.4	240.3	16.7	257.0
** Total (Lux10) Antiques/Auctions			332	223	292	9	302	4 559	74	4 633

Table 8.5 continued

Clocks and Watches									
Accurist watches	Maslin Rees Fitton/Billet	542.9	–	–	–	–	–	564.7	564.7
Audemar Piquet watch	Overseas Agency	11.6	9.2	6.0		6.0	131.6	–	131.6
Avia watches	Still Price Court Twivy D's	47.1	–	–	–	–	202.1	–	202.1
Baume and Merc watches	RPG Advertising	11.0	–	3.8	–	3.8	76.8	–	76.8
Blancpain watches	Overseas Agency	10.6	9.4	9.5	–	9.5	131.7	–	131.7
Braun Reflex Control alarm clock	Harris Kemp/C.I.A.	433.7	18.1	–	–	–	–	451.8	451.8
Burberry watches	Media Marketing	24.6	–	–	–	–	81.4	–	81.4
Casio Data Bank watch	Sears & Nalson	50.9	–	–	–	–	78.1	–	78.1
Casio watches	Sears & Nalson	143.7	–	–	–	–	289.4	–	289.4
Citizen watches	Lintas: London/BBVS	662.7	91.4	–	–	–	773.1	368.4	1 141.5
Concord watches	Overseas Agency	–	–	–	–	–	102.5	–	102.5
Corum watches		3.2	–	–	–	–	82.7	–	82.7
Dunhill watches	BMP Davidson Pearce	42.3	3.6	–	–	–	135.0	–	135.0
Ebel watches	Overseas Agency/F J F	18.6	4.1	–	–	–	162.7	–	162.7
Eterna watches	Saatchi & Saatchi/Zenit	–	–	–	–	–	79.7	–	79.7
Flik Flak watches	Overseas Agency/BMP BU	15.4	–	–	–	–	94.2	133.2	227.4
Garrard watches		29.4	–	–	–	–	48.0	–	48.0
Gucci watches	H Q Partnership/AMS(L)	44.8	76.7	65.7	–	65.7	349.5	56.9	406.4
Hana watches	Hilton Advertising G/M Grp.	2.5	–	–	–	–	42.6	2.5	45.1
Jean Lassale watches	Roose O.W.D.	23.3	1.7	–	–	–	109.6	–	109.6
Longines watches	Overseas Agency	75.4	–	–	–	–	331.8	–	331.8
Lorus watches	Roose O.W.D.	32.2	–	–	–	–	138.7	–	138.7
Noblia Citizen watches	Lintas: London	46.7	–	–	–	–	58.7	–	58.7
Omega watches	*Overseas Agency/Jarvis	78.4	–	4.3	–	4.3	828.7	–	828.7
Patek Phillipe watch	Overseas Agency	27.2	–	–	–	–	216.0	–	216.0

Table 8.5 concluded

Piaget watches	RPG Advertising	14.6	3.7	3.2	–	3.2	89.9	–	89.9
Pulsar watches	Burkitt Weinreich Bryant	221.2	16.9	–	–	–	355.4	–	355.4
Rado watches	Media Reach Advertising	54.9	3.9	1.4	–	1.4	234.4	30.1	264.5
Raymond Weil watches	Reid Walker	59.5	–	–	–	–	273.6	–	273.6
Rolex watches	J Walter Thompson London	37.4	26.6	28.0	–	28.0	482.8	–	482.8
Rotary watches	KHBB/Zenit	288.0	–	–	–	–	238.7	259.7	498.5
Seiko watches	Burkitt Weinreich Bryant	217.6	4.8	–	–	–	758.7	–	758.7
Sekonda watches	Gold Greenlees Trott	309.6	–	–	–	–	–	842.4	842.4
Swatch watches	Overseas Agency/Jarvis	4.0	6.7	–	–	–	97.4	1 251.2	1 348.7
Tag Heuer watches	Bartle Bogle Hegarty	30.4	–	–	–	–	229.8	–	229.8
Timex watches	Ogilvy & Mather Partners	146.7	–	–	–	–	459.1	–	459.1
Tissot Rock watches	Travis Dale	–	–	–	–	–	–	222.2	222.2
Tissot watches	Travis Dale	120.9	–	–	–	–	256.9	378.2	635.1
Zenith watches	Overseas Agency	1.8	–	–	–	–	44.1	–	44.1
** Watches Misc **		14.8	–	5.6	–	5.6	105.1	–	105.1
Sub-threshold Brands 21		124.0	6.8	6.8	–	6.8	349.3	–	349.3
** Total (Lux20) Clocks and Watches		4 023	283	134	–	134	8 519	4 561	13 081

The Media Register bases its press statistics on rate cards but its TV expenditure data is based on a complicated technique linked to the TV airtime market-place. This technique claims to produce more accurate figures for individual brand expenditure although some brands will spend slightly more and some slightly less than the calculation depending on various market-place factors. As a result, both MEAL and Media Register statistics can only be estimates.

For statistics on the advertising sector in general, the major source is the Advertising Association, although its publications are available from NTC Publications. The Association began publishing statistics in 1948 and now has a range of annual and quarterly series.

Its *Quarterly Survey of Advertising Expenditure* covers expenditure through the press, television, radio, posters, cinema and direct mail. Expenditure on the broader area of sales promotion and exhibitions and fairs is excluded since only a proportion of expenditure in these areas can be classed as advertising. Advertising expenditure by specific industry and product sectors is also covered.

An *Advertising Statistics Yearbook* includes statistics by media type plus data on product sectors, prices, top advertisers, agencies, complaints, attitudes and international trends. Historical data is included.

Both of these publications bring together data from various sources, including MEAL, but the Advertising Association also carries out its own regular surveys of actual advertising expenditure as opposed to rate card costs. A quarterly *Forecast of Advertising Expenditure* in the UK has forecasts for the main media categories and there are forecasts of expenditure for the main product sectors. There is a companion title giving a *European Advertising and Media Forecast*.

Other sources of advertising data can be the agencies themselves. Saatchi & Saatchi, for example, publishes regular *Advertising Expenditure Forecasts* and an annual *European Market & Media Fact* book. As well as expenditure data, many research companies provide services which measure advertising effectiveness, advertising reach and consumer awareness of, and attitudes to advertising.

General sources

While buying detailed market research results can be expensive, there are some general publications which include basic data from market research sources and these are available relatively cheaply.

NTC Publications publishes a series of annual pocketbooks, in association with the Advertising Association, for around £14 per book. These combine official statistics with market research and other data. Titles include the *Marketing Pocketbook*, the *Media Pocketbook*, the *Lifestyle Pocketbook* and the *Regional Marketing Pocketbook*.

Since 1989, JICNARS, in association with Research Services Ltd, has been publishing an annual *Marketing Data Book* including summary demographic and socio-economic data from the JICNARS survey.

The market survey publishers described in Chapter 6, such as Euromonitor, Mintel and Market Assessment, include the summary results of original research in many of their reports.

The individual independent TV companies produce marketing manuals of their areas, updated every few years, with demographic and consumer data taken mainly from market research sources. Most of these manuals are aimed at potential advertisers but they have wider applications and are usually available free from the company concerned.

Trade journals and the marketing press reproduce data from original research in regular features and articles. The weekly, *Electrical and Radio Trading* (ERT), for example, has regular articles on specific products with data from AGB's Lek-Trak service mentioned earlier in this chapter.

Since 1932, general data on newspaper, journal and magazine circulation has come from Audit Bureau of Circulation Ltd (ABC), an independent organization controlled by its membership of advertisers, agencies and publishers. The company audits the circulation, that is, the net sales of members' publications and publishes the figures twice a year. Verified Free Distribution (VFD) is a subsidiary company auditing the circulation of free newspapers and other titles.

British Rate and Data (BRAD) is a standard reference source for the marketing and advertising sectors. It is published monthly and contains information, including advertising rates and circulation figures from ABC and VFD, on specific UK media.

9 Statistical Examples

The examples given below are intended as brief illustrations of some of the problems associated with using published statistics. Some examples also emphasize that different figures on the same subject can be generated by different sources. Further details on the problems associated with using particular statistical series are given in the relevant subject chapters. Ultimately, the user must decide on the most appropriate source.

Example 1: Balance of payments data

Estimates of the current account of the balance of payments are published monthly in press releases (see Chapter 5) but these figures are subsequently revised. There are also quarterly trade figures but these are also only estimates which are revised later. The problem is that revisions to the figures can continue for years as new information is obtained and the published figures are regularly changing.

Table 9.1 shows the changes to the 1985 current account of the balance of payments figures which have taken place between May 1986 and December 1990. The total figure is based on a combination of visible and invisible trade and, mainly due to revisions in the invisibles figure, the total had been revised 21 times up to December 1990.

Table 9.1 Current account of the balance of payments: the 1985 balances – changing figures 1986–1990, £ million

Time of Estimate	Visible	Invisible	Current
May 1986	−2 068	+5 020	+2 952
June 1986	−2 068	+5 831	+3 763
August 1986	−2 111	+5 713	+3 602
December 1986	−2 111	+5 660	+3 549
February 1987	−2 178	+5 660	+3 482
March 1987	−2 178	+5 124	+2 946
May 1987	−2 178	+5 628	+3 450
July 1987	−2 178	+5 097	+2 919
December 1987	−2 178	+5 066	+2 888
February 1988	−2 190	+5 457	+3 267
March 1988	−2 190	+5 465	+275
July 1988	−2 190	+5 463	+3 273
September 1988	−2 346	+5 683	+3 337
March 1989	−2 346	+5 701	+3 355
August 1989	−3 131	+6 335	+3 204
October 1989	−3 132	+6 335	+3 203
December 1989	−3 132	+6 293	+3 161
January 1990	−3 131	+6 293	+3 162
February 1990	−3 128	+6 293	+3 165
August 1990	−3 128	+6 095	+2 967
December 1990	−3 345	+6 095	+2 750

Source: CSO *Press Releases* and *Economic Trends*

Example 2: Gross Domestic Product statistics

There are three measures of GDP: an expenditure measure, an income measure, and an output measure (see Chapter 5). An average GDP figure, GDP(A), from the three measures, is also produced. In

Table 9.2 GDP Measures – Quarterly Figures, 1986–1988

Volume Indices at Constant Prices

	Expenditure GDP(E)	Income GDP(I)	Output GDP(O)	Average GDP(A)
1980=100				
1986:				
quarter 1	110.9	111.8	111.4	111.4
quarter 2	111.5	112.6	112.9	112.3
quarter 3	111.5	112.5	114.5	112.8
quarter 4	113.0	115.3	115.2	114.5
1987:				
quarter 1	115.3	117.0	116.4	116.2
quarter 2	114.9	119.0	118.1	117.4
quarter 3	118.0	120.7	120.8	119.8
quarter 4	118.1	121.2	121.8	120.6
1988:				
quarter 1	119.1	122.5	122.5	121.4
1985=100				
1988:				
quarter 2	108.1	111.5	112.8	110.8
quarter 3	107.2	112.1	113.6	112.4
quarter 4	111.5	111.8	113.5	112.3

The initial figures above are later revised. For example, the 3rd quarter 1988 figures were revised at the end of the year and have been revised on a number of occasions since. By June 1991, the revised figures for the 3rd quarter 1988 were:

GDP(E) = 113.1, GDP(I) = 113.6, GDP(O) = 113.1, GDP(A) = 113.3.

theory, they are all equal but, in practice, they are likely to be slightly different because they are calculated in different ways. In the late

1980s, these differences became particularly large with the expenditure measure lagging behind the other two measures. With three diverging GDP measures, calculating growth becomes problematic and confusing.

The figures are also revised in later periods. Quarterly figures for 1986 to 1988 are included in Table 9.2 and they clearly show divergences in the three measures in 1986 to 1988 with the widest divergence between the expenditure and output measure in the third quarter of 1988. The figures come from the first quarterly published figures for each period appearing in *Economic Trends*.

Example 3: Population statistics

Local population statistics are produced by central government and local authorities and the different methods used produce different results. The most comprehensive survey is the Population Census and this produces two main figures. For example, in the 1981 census, the usually resident population of the county of Hampshire was given as 1 442 600. The enumerated population of the county was the actual number of people present in the county on census night and this was 1 466 400. The mid-year estimate of the population of Hampshire for 1981 was 1 479 500 but in May 1983, following the publication of the census data, the 1981 mid-year estimate was revised to 1 488 000. The local county council also produced population figures, based on an 'enhanced electoral register survey' and the council's population figure for 1981 was 1 453 300.

Example 4: Socio-economic data

The various government socio-economic surveys are conducted using different samples and questioning techniques (see Chapter 4 for further details). Although the three main surveys, the FES, GHS and NFS, specialize in particular subjects, there is also a degree of overlap. Both the FES (Family Expenditure Survey) and the National Food Survey (NFS) collect data on food expenditure but the nature of the results are different.

FES results are usually expressed in terms of the average weekly household expenditure. In 1989, survey results showed that the average weekly expenditure on food per household was £41.67p. There is also data on specific foods. For example, the average weekly household expenditure on potatoes was £1.30.

The NFS also collects data on food expenditure but expresses the results in terms of the amount spent per person per week. Expenditure per person per week on food was £11.50 in 1989 with expenditure on potatoes per week at 25.18 pence. Consumption figures are also included in the NFS.

Example 5: Market data – video recorders

In some markets, the problem for the user is that there is so much data available that selecting the most reliable, and most suitable, for a particular requirement can be difficult. The market for video recorders (VCRs) is covered by various sources including official statistics, market research data, trade association data and statistics from companies in the market (see Chapter 6 for general details of these sources). Most of these use different methods to collect the data and the user must also be aware that the scope of the surveys and definitions used also vary, with some covering retail sales, manufacturer's sales, consumer offtake, trade deliveries etc. Just a selection of sources are given below.

Official statistics are published in *Business Monitor PAS 3454* (previously *PQ 3454*). Sales statistics refer to sales by UK manufacturers only but import and export data are also included. The sales figures have been published separately since 1986 and a value figure is given but no quantity figure. Import and export statistics are given in both values and volumes.

An estimate of the UK market can be obtained by finding the sales and subtracting exports, then adding imports. The sales figures are usually revised – the first provisional figure for sales in 1988 was £281.9 million but this was later revised to £291.7 million.

The British Radio and Electronic Equipment Manufacturers Association (BREMA) publishes quarterly statistics for VCRs but the data specifically cover deliveries to the trade and figures are usually only expressed in units.

The AGB Lek-Trak service has aggregate figures for retail sales of VCRs through shops and these figures are regularly reported in the journal *Electrical and Radio Trading*. Figures are usually given in values, at retail selling prices, and volumes.

Table 9.3 VCR market in 1988 – a selection of the range of statistics available

Business Monitor PAS 3454	
1988 Sales by UK Manufacturers	£291.7 million
1988 Market Estimate	
(above sales – exports + imports)	£455.2 million
BREMA Quarterly Statistics	
1988 Trade Deliveries to the UK Market	2 400 000 units
UK Made Number of Above Total	882 000 units
Ferguson's 'UK Consumer Electronics Market'	
Consumer Offtake of VCRs	2 350 000 units
AGB Lek-Trak, reported in *Electrical & Radio Trading*, June 1989	
Retail Sales through Electrical Outlets	
(year to April 1989)	£590.99 million
	1 895 800 units
Euromonitor Report in *Market Research Great Britain*, September 1990	
Sales at Retail Selling Prices	£706 million
	2 200 000 units
Mintel Report, December 1990	
Consumer Offtake of VCRs	£773 million
	2 400 000
Key Note Report, 1991	
Consumer Offtake of VCRs	£773 million
	2 358 000

The electronics company, Ferguson, carries out an annual survey of the consumer electronics market with a volume figure for consumer offtake of VCRs, based on original Ferguson research and the BREMA figures. Market survey publishers, including Mintel, Key Note and Euromonitor, publish reports on VCRs with calculations using data from the above sources plus some original market research.

Not surprisingly, the figures from all these sources can vary considerably and some selected examples are given in Table 9.3.

Example 6: Market data – frozen foods and central heating

Using Business Monitors to obtain market data can be time-consuming particularly in markets with different groups and types of products. For example, obtaining a figure for the frozen food market would involve scanning various Business Monitors as individual Monitors cover particular foods, such as fruit and vegetable products, fish products, ice-cream, bacon curing and meat products, and poultry and poultry products. No one monitor gives the total figure for frozen foods sales. More appropriate sources for a market figure are likely to be market research reports and trade associations.

A number of Business Monitors cover domestic heating equipment and these would be potential sources for data on domestic central heating systems. For example, *PAS3165 Domestic heating & cooking appliances*, *PAS 3205 Boilers and process plant fabrications*, *PAS 3460 Domestic electrical appliances*. In fact, only domestic central heating boilers are included as a separate heading in *PAS 3205* and building up a picture of the total central heating sector is impossible.

More appropriate sources are trade associations and market research surveys. The Building Services Research and Information Association, for example, publishes regular statistics on the domestic central heating market by type, that is gas, electricity, oil etc., and forecasts of the market in the quarterly *BSRIA Statistics Bulletin*.

Example 7: Import/export data

Statistics on product imports and exports are produced monthly from traders' forms. These figures are often revised at the end of the year (see Chapter 6 for further details).

When examining the trade in a particular product between two countries, it is unlikely that the export figures from one country will match the import figures from another country. Time delays, differences in product definitions, exchange rate fluctuations, changes in the administrative systems and genuine mistakes in

Table 9.4 UK export statistics and French import statistics showing the trade between UK and France in plastic syringes

1986–1989 **Figures in 000s of ECUs**

	UK Exports	*French Imports*
1986	3 236	3 830
1987	2 340	4 002
1988	4 346	4 640
1989	4 067	3 892

completing forms will all affect the figures. Some of the products exported from one country may not actually be imported into the original country of destination and they may be re-exported to a third country.

The figures in Table 9.4 show the published figures for the exports of plastic syringes from the UK to France and the published figures for the imports of plastic syringes into France from the UK. The figures are taken from Eurostat, the statistical office of the EC, which brings together the published trade data from EC member countries. The figures have been converted to a common currency, the ECU.

The UK and French figures seem to disagree on the amount of trade between the two countries. In 1987, particularly, UK statistics showed a fall in UK exports of syringes to France but French import statistics showed a significant rise in French imports of syringes from the UK. Many of these differences can be explained by the points noted above but, as a general rule, one country's export figures should not be used as the sole source of data on another country's imports.

Example 8: Unemployment

The two main official measures of unemployment use different methods and definitions (see Chapter 7 for further details). One unemployment figure comes from a survey of the labour force, the Labour Force Survey and its definition is based on that developed by the International Labour Office (ILO). The other unemployment

Table 9.5 Unemployment statistics – a comparison of LFS and figures from unemployment benefit offices (UBOs), 1984–1989

Great Britain, spring each year millions

	1984	1985	1986	1987	1988	1989
LFS	3.09	2.97	2.97	2.88	2.38	1.98
UBO*+ (unadjusted)	2.98	3.13	3.17	2.95	2.41	1.78
UBO*+ (seasonally adjusted)	2.77	2.91	2.99	2.80	2.28	1.75

* The unadjusted claimant count is not fully consistent over the periods shown. Consistent comparisons over time, allowing for discontinuities, can be made using the seasonally adjusted series (although this excludes under 18s).
\+ Weighted averages of monthly claimant count to cover survey period

figure is generated by the administrative system at unemployment benefit offices and this monthly series has been the subject of various coverage and definition changes in recent years.

Both series produce different results, as Table 9.5 shows. In 1984, the LFS unemployment figure was higher than the benefit offices figure; in 1985 and 1986 the position was reversed, and in 1989, the LFS figure was again higher. In intervening years, either figure could be higher according to which series of UBO statistics was used, the seasonally adjusted or unadjusted series.

Example 9: Advertising data

Advertising expenditure for specific brands and products are available from two competing services, MEAL and the Media Register. The services use different methods to estimate expenditure and cover different media so the final totals for specific products vary between the services from month to month and year to year (see Chapter 8 for further details).

For example, in February 1990 MEAL estimated total advertising expenditure for clocks and watches at £194 000 while the Media Register estimated the total at £184 000. Despite the differences in the methods used to calculate the figures, the divergences in the figures never seem to become that great. In the year to the end of February 1990, MEAL's estimate of total advertising expenditure on clocks and watches was £15 395 000 and Media Register's was £15 299 000.

Appendix 1: UK business statistics – contacts and addresses

1. Statistical publishers and services

A list of the main sources noted in the text.

Abacus Data Services (UK) Ltd
Causeway House, 24 South Drive, Coulsdon, Surrey CR3 2BG
Tel: 081 763 1000 Fax: 081 681 2440

Advertising Association
Abford House, 15 Wilton Road, London SW1V 1NJ
Tel: 071 828 2772 Fax: 071 931 0376

Association of British Chambers of Commerce (ABCC)
212A Shaftesbury Avenue, London WC2 8EW
Tel: 071 240 5831 Fax: 071 379 6331

Association of Market Survey Organisations (AMSO)
Mulberry House, 36 Smith Square, London SW1P 3HL
Tel: 071 222 8181

Audit Bureau of Circulation (ABC)
13 Wimpole Street, London W1M 7AB
Tel: 071 631 1343

Audits of Great Britain (AGB)
The Research Centre, West Gate, W5 1UA
Tel: 081 566 8255

Bank of England
Threadneedle Street, London EC2R 8AH
Tel: 071 601 4444

BBC Enterprises
1 Portland Place, London W1A 1AA
Tel: 071 927 5998 Fax: 071 637 0398

British Bankers Association
10 Lombard Street, London EC3V 9EL
Tel: 071 626 8486 Fax 071 283 7037

British Market Research Bureau (BMRB)
53 The Mall, Ealing, London W5 3TE
Tel: 081 567 3060

British Rate and Data (BRAD)
1A Chalk Lane, Cockfosters Road, Barnet EN4 0BU
Tel: 081 441 6644

British Tourist Authority
Thames Tower, Blacks Road, London W6 9EL
Tel: 081 846 9000

Broadcasters' Audience Research Bureau (BARB)
Glenthorne House, Glenthorne Road, London W6 0LG
Tel: 081 741 9110

Business and Trade Statistics Ltd
Lancaster House, More Lane, Esher, Surrey KT10 8AP
Tel: 0372 463121 Fax: 0372 469847

Business Media Research Committee (BMRC)
c/o Research Services Ltd, Research Services House, Elmgrove Road, Harrow HA1 2QG
Tel: 081 861 6000 Fax: 081 861 5515

Business Strategies Ltd
10 Kendrick Mews, London SW7 3HG
Tel: 071 823 7399

CACI Ltd
Regent House, 89 Kingsway, London WC2B 6RH
Tel: 071 528 7980 Fax: 071 528 7988

Cambridge Econometrics Ltd
PO Box 114, St Andrew's Street, Cambridge CB2 3AX
Tel: 0223 460760 Fax: 0223 66274

CCN Marketing
Talbot House, Talbot Street, Nottingham NG1 5HF
Tel: 0602 410888 Fax: 0602 415416

CDMS
JM Centre, Old Hall Street, Liverpool L70 1AB
Tel: 051 235 3298

Central Statistical Office (CSO)
Great George Street, London SW1P 3AQ
Tel: 071 270 6357 (public inquiries), 071 270 6357 (CSO Databank)

Central Statistical Office (CSO)
Government Buildings, Cardiff Road, Newport, Gwent NP9 1XG
Tel: 0633 812973 Fax: 0633 812599

Central Statistical Office (CSO)
Branch E2B, PO Box 1333, Millbank Tower, Millbank, London SW1P 4QQ
Tel: 071 217 4245/4255 (FES inquiries)

Central Statistical Office (CSO)
CSO Statcall (telephone service) Tel: 0839 338, plus the following number:
RPI: 337
Monthly trade figures: 338
Balance of payments (q): 339

PSBR: 340
Index of industrial production: 341
Producer prices: 342
Retail sales: 343
Credit business: 344
GDP: 345

Chartered Institute of Public Finance & Accountancy (CIPFA)
3 Robert Street, London WC2N 6BH
Tel: 071 895 8823 Fax: 071 895 8825

Cinema Advertising Association
127 Wardour Street, London W1V 4AD
Tel: 071 439 9531 Fax: 071 439 2395

CMT Ltd
Computerised Marketing Technologies Ltd
Teddington House, 67 Broad Street, Teddington TW11 8QZ
Tel: 081 977 8737 Fax: 081 943 3697

Confederation of British Industry (CBI)
Centre Point, 103 New Oxford Street, London WC1A 1DU
Tel: 071 379 7400 Fax: 071 240 1578

Data Star
D/S Marketing Ltd
Plaza Suite, 114 Jermyn Street, London SW1Y 6HJ
Tel: 071 930 5503 Fax: 071 930 2581

Datastream International
Monmouth House, 58 City Road, London EC1Y 2AE
Tel: 071 251 3002

Department of Agriculture For Northern Ireland
Economics and Statistics Division
Room 817, Dundonald House, Belfast BT4 3SB

Department of Economic Development (Northern Ireland)
Statistics Branch
Netherleigh House, Massey Avenue, Belfast BT4 2JP
Tel: 0232 63244

Department of Employment
Caxton House, Tothill Street, London SW1H 9NF
Tel: 071 273 3000

Department of Energy
Economics and Statistics Division
Room 1483, Thames House South, Millbank, London SW1P 4QJ
Tel: 071 238 2606

Department of the Environment
2 Marsham Street, London SW1P 3EB
Tel: 071 276 4003

Department of the Environment
Publications Sales Unit
Building 1, Victoria Road, Ruislip, Middlesex HA4 0NZ
Tel: 071 841 3425

Department of Finance and Personnel (Northern Ireland)
Policy Planning and Research Unit
Stormont, Belfast BT4 3SW
Tel: 0232 63210

Department of Trade and Industry
Ashdown House, 123 Victoria Street, London SW1E 6RB
Tel: 071 215 6218

Department of Transport
Romney House, 43 Marsham Street, London SW1P 3PY
Tel: 071 276 8520

Department of Transport
Publications Sales Unit
Building 1, Victoria Road, South Ruislip, Middlesex HA4 0NZ
Tel: 081 841 3425

Donovan Data Systems
Berger House, 7 Farm Street, London W1X 7RB
Tel: 071 629 7654 Fax: 071 493 0239

DRI Europe
Wimbledon Bridge House, Hartfield Road, Wimbledon SW19 3RU
Tel: 081 543 1234

Dun & Bradstreet Ltd
Holmers Farm Way, High Wycombe, Bucks HP12 4UL
Tel: 0494 422000 Fax: 0494 423708

Economist Intelligence Unit (EIU)
40 Duke Street, London W1A 1DW
Tel: 071 493 6711 Fax: 071 499 9767

Employment Department
Statistical Services Division A1
60 Exchange Road, Watford WD1 7HH
Tel: 0923 228500

Employment Department
Skills and Enterprise Network
Room W801, Moorfoot, Sheffield, S1 4PQ
Tel: 0742 594318

ESRC Data Archive
University of Essex, Colchester CO4 3SQ
Tel: 0206 872319

Euromonitor plc
87–88 Turnmill Street, London EC1M 5QU
Tel: 071 251 8024 Fax: 071 608 3149

Eurostat
Information Office
L–2920 Luxembourg
Tel: 4301 4567

Financial Times Business Information
7th Floor, 50–64 Broadway, London SW1H 0DB
Tel: 071 799 2002 Fax: 071 799 2259

FT Profile
PO Box 12, Sunbury-on-Thames, Middlesex TW16 7UD
Tel: 0932 761444 Fax: 0932 781425

General Register Office for Northern Ireland
Oxford House, 49–55 Chichester Street, Belfast BT1 4HL
Tel: 0232 235211

General Register Office for Scotland
Ladywood House, Ladywood Road, Edinburgh EH12 7TF
Tel: 031 334 0380

Government Actuary's Department
22 Kingsway, London WC2B 6LE
Tel: 071 242 6828

Guy Consterdine Associates
Midelney House, Fairfield Lane, West End, Woking, Surrey
GU24 9QX
Fax: 0276 858274

Harvest
63 St Martin's Lane, London WC2N 4JT
Tel: 071 836 8633 Fax: 071 240 2602

Hay Management Consultants
52 Grosvenor Gardens, London SW1W 0AU
Tel: 071 730 0833 Fax: 071 730 8193

Henley Centre
2–4 Tudor Street, Blackfriars, London EC4Y 0AA
Tel: 071 353 9961 Fax: 071 353 2899

HM Customs and Excise
New King's Beam House, 22 Upper Ground, London SE1 9PJ
Tel: 071 620 1313

HM Treasury
Parliament Street, London SW1P 3AG
Tel: 071 270 4860

HMSO Books
PO Box 276, London SW8 5DT
Tel: 071 873 8499

Hoare Govett
8 Broadgate, London EC2
Tel: 071 601 0101

Holborn Research Services (HRS)
Grosvenor House, Grosvenor Gardens, London SW1W 0BS
Tel: 071 630 5033 Fax: 071 828 3642

ICC
Field House, 72 Oldfield Road, Hampton, Middlesex TW12 1BR
Tel: 081 783 0755 Fax: 081 783 1940

Incomes Data Services Ltd
193 St John Street, London EC1V 4LS
Tel: 071 250 3434

Industrial Relations Services (IRS)
18 Highbury Place, London N5
Tel: 071 354 5858

Inland Revenue
Somerset House, Strand, London WC2R 1LB
Tel: 071 438 7370

Institute of Directors
116 Pall Mall, London SW1Y 5ED
Tel: 071 839 1233 Fax: 071 930 1949

Institute for Employment Research
University of Warwick Gibbett Hill Road, Coventry CV4 7AL
Tel: 0203 523523

Institute of Practitioners in Advertising (IPA)
44 Belgrave Square, London SW1X 8QS
Tel: 071 235 7020 Fax: 071 245 9904

Interactive Market Systems (UK) Ltd (IMS)
Grosvenor Gardens House, Grosvenor Gardens, London SW1W 0BS
Tel: 071 630 5033 Fax: 071 828 3642

International Stock Exchange
Old Broad Street, London EC2N 1HP
Tel: 071 588 2355 Fax: 071 256 8972

I P Sharp Associates Ltd
10 Dean Farrar Street, London SW1H 0DX
Tel: 071 222 7023

Joint Industry Committee for National Readership Surveys (JICNARS)
44 Belgrave Square, London SW1X 8QS
Tel: 071 235 7020 Fax: 071 245 9904

Key Note Publications Ltd
Field House, 72 Oldfield Road, Hampton, Middlesex TW12 2HQ
Tel: 081 783 0755 Fax: 081 783 1940

Labour Research Department (LRD)
78 Blackfriars Road, London SE1 8HF
Tel: 071 928 3649

McCarthy Information Ltd
Manor House, Ash Walk, Warminster, Wiltshire BA12 8PY
Tel: 0985 215151 Fax: 0985 217479

Macroeconomic Modelling Bureau
University of Warwick, Gibbett Hill Road, Coventry CV4 7AL
Tel: 0203 523523

MAID Systems Ltd
Maid House, 26 Baker Street, London W1M 1DF
Tel: 071 935 6460

Manpower
Manpower House, 270/272 High Street, Slough SL1 1LJ
Tel: 0753 73111 Fax: 0753 824524

Maritime and Distribution Systems (Overseas Trade Data)
28 City Road, Chester CH1 3AE
Tel: 0244 346198 Fax: 0244 348471

Market Assessment Publications Ltd
2 Duncan Terrace, London N1 8BZ
Tel: 071 278 9517 Fax: 071 278 6246

Market Location Ltd
1 Warwick Street, Leamington Spa CV32 5LW
Tel: 0926 450388 Fax: 0926 450592

Media Expenditure Analysis Ltd (MEAL)
63 St Martin's Lane, London WC2N 4JT
Tel: 071 240 1903/6 Fax: 071 240 2602

Media Register
Register House, 4 Holford Yard, London WX1X 9HF
Tel: 071 833 1212

Ministry of Agriculture, Fisheries and Food (MAFF)
West Block, Whitehall Place, London SW1A 2HN
Tel: 071 270 8562 (National Food Survey)

Ministry of Agriculture, Fisheries and Food (MAFF)
Publications Section
Room A615, Epsom Road, Guildford GU1 2LD
Tel: 0483 68121

MORI
32 Old Queen Street, London SW1H 9HP
Tel: 071 222 0232

National Economic Development Office (NEDO)
Joint Forecasting Committee of the NEDC, Construction Industry Sector Group
Millbank Tower, Millbank, London SW1P 4QX
Tel: 071 217 4004

National Health Service Central Register (OPCS Dept.)
Smedley Hydro, Trafalger Road, Southport PR8 2HH

Nielsen Marketing Research
Nielsen House, Headington, Oxford OX9 9RX
Tel: 0865 742742 Fax: 0865 742222

National Institute of Economic and Social Research (NIESR)
2 Dean Trench Street, Smith Square, London SW1P 3HE
Tel: 071 222 7665

National On-Line Manpower Information System (NOMIS)
Unit 3, Mountjoy Research Centre, Durham University, Durham DH1 3SW
Tel: 091 374 2468 Fax: 091 374 3741

NOP Market Research
Tower House, Southampton Street, London SO2 9PH
Tel: 071 836 1511 Fax: 071 836 2052

NTC Publications Ltd
PO Box 691, 22–24 Bell Street, Henley-on-Thames, RG9 2BZ
Tel: 0491 574671 Fax 0491 571188

Office of Population, Censuses and Surveys (OPCS)
St Catherines House, 10 Kingsway, London WC2B 6JP

Office of Population, Censuses and Surveys (OPCS)
Titchfield, Fareham, Hampshire PO15 5RR
Tel: 0329 42511, ext 296 (population census), ext 3065 (population estimates)

Pergamon Financial Data Services (PFDS)
Paulton House, 8 Shepherdess Walk, London N1 7LB
Tel: 071 490 0049

Pinpoint Analysis Ltd
Mercury House, 117 Waterloo Road, London SE1 8UL
Tel: 071 928 1874 Fax: 071 633 0402

Population Census Office (Northern Ireland)
5A Frederick Street, Belfast BT1 2LW
Tel: 0232 244711

Projection 2000 Ltd
27 Belfast Road, London N16 6UN
Tel: 081 806 3139

Property Intelligence plc
Ingram House, 13–15 John Adam Street, London WC2N 6LD
Tel: 071 839 7684 Fax: 071 839 1060

Remuneration Economics
51 Portland Road, Kingston-upon-Thames, KT1 2SH
Tel: 081 549 8726 Fax: 081 541 5705

Research Services Ltd (RSL)
Research Services House, Elmgrove Road, Harrow, Middlesex HA1 2QG
Tel: 081 861 6000 Fax: 081 861 5515

Reuters
85 Fleet Street, London EC4P 4AJ
Tel: 071 250 1122

Scottish Office
Library Sales
Room 2/65, New St Andrews House, Edinburgh EH1 3TG

Scrimgeour Vickers
Regis House, King William Street, London EC4
Tel: 071 234 5600

Social and Community Planning Research (SCPR)
35 Northampton Square, London EC1V 0AX
Tel: 071 250 1866

Social Surveys (Gallup Poll) Ltd
Gallup House, 307 Finchley Road, London NW3 6EH
Tel: 071 794 0461 Fax: 071 435 5947

Telmar Communications
Southbank Technopark, 90 London Road, London SE1 6LN
Tel: 071 922 8816 Fax: 071 261 9724

Unit for Retail Planning Information (URPI)
7 Southern Court, South Street, Reading RG1 4QS
Tel: 0734 588181 Fax: 0734 597637

WEFA Group Ltd
Ebury Gate, 23 Lower Belgrave Street, London SW1W 0NW
Tel: 071 730 8171/8172

Welsh Office
Economic and Statistical Service Division
Crown Buildings, Cathays Park, Cardiff CF1 3NQ

2. Selected statistical libraries

British Library Science Reference and Information Service (SRIS)
25 Southampton Buildings, Chancery Lane, London WC2A 1AW
Tel: 071 323 7454

Collection of UK official business statistics and some non-official data including market research reports, trade association reports and trade journals.

Central Statistical Office Library
Government Buildings, Cardiff Road, Newport NP9 1XG
Tel: 0633 812973 Fax: 0633 812599

Collection of official and some non-official statistics. Also supplies individual copies of Business Monitors.

Export Market Information Centre (EMIC)
Ashdown House, 123 Victoria Street, London SW1E 6RB
Tel: 071 215 5000

An international collection of statistics which is open to the public. As it is a library intended for exporters, its coverage of UK statistics has been reduced dramatically in the last few years.

Official Publications and Social Sciences Information Service
Great Russell Street, London WC1B 3DG
Tel: 071 636 1544

Collection of official titles.

OPCS Library
Office of Population Censuses and Surveys
St Catherines House, 10 Kingsway, London WC2B 6JP
Tel: 071 242 0262

Collection of population statistics, including some census material from overseas. A prior appointment must be made to use the library.

Warwick University Business Information Service
University of Warwick Library
Gibbett Hill Road, Coventry CV4 7AL
Tel: 0203 523051 Fax: 0203 524211

Collection of UK and international statistics, used as the basis for a fee-based information service.

3. General organizations and groups interested in published statistics

Committee of Librarians and Statisticians
The Library Association
7 Ridgmount Street, London WC1E 7AE
Tel: 071 636 7543 Fax: 071 436 7218

Royal Statistical Society (RSS)
25 Enford Street, London W1H 2BH
Tel: 071 723 5882

Statistics Users Council (SUC)
c/o Business and Trade Statistics
Lancaster House, More Lane, Esher, Surrey KT10 8AP
Tel: 0372 463121 Fax: 0372 469847

Appendix 2: Selected abbreviations and acronyms

ABC: Audit Bureau of Circulation
ACORN: A Classification of Residential Neighbourhoods (geo-demographic classification)
BARB: Broadcasters Audience Research Board
BMRC: Business Media Research Committee
BRAD: British Rate and Data
BSO: Business Statistics Office, now part of the Central Statistical Office
CAVIAR: Cinema and Video Industry Audience Research
CODOT: Classification of Occupations and Directory of Occupational Titles
CSO: Central Statistical Office
ED: Enumeration District (administrative unit for the population census)
EUROSTAT: Statistical Office of the European Commission
FES: Family Expenditure Survey
FOOTSIE: FT-SE 100 Share Index
GDP: Gross Domestic Product
GRO: General Register Office
GSS: Government Statistical Service
GHS: General Household Survey
HS: Harmonized Commodity Description and Coding System (product imports and exports)

JICNARS: Joint Industry Committee for National Readership Surveys
JICRAR: Joint Industry Committee for Radio Audience Research
JICREG: Joint Industry Committee for Regional Press Readership Research
LFS: Labour Force Survey
M0 – M5: Various measures of the money supply
MOSAIC: Geo-demographic classification scheme
NACE: Nomenclature générale des activités économiques dans les Communautés européennes (industrial classification scheme)
NES: New Earnings Survey
NFS: National Food Survey
NOMIS: National On-Line Manpower Information System
NRS: National Readership Survey (run by JICNARS)
NSS: National Shoppers Survey
OPCS: Office of Population Censuses and Surveys
OSCAR: Outdoor Site Classification and Audience Research
PAF: Postcode Address File
PIN: Pinpoint Identified neighbourhoods (geo-demographic classification)
PPI: Producer Price Index
PRODCOM: Scheme of Harmonized European Product Sales Statistics
RPI: Retail Price Index
RPIAC: Retail Price Index Advisory Committee
SAR : Sample of Anonymous Records (population census)
SAS: Small Area Statistics (population census)
SIC: Standard Industrial Classification
SITC: Standard International Trade Classification
SOC: Standard Occupational Classification
SUPERPROFILE: Geo-demographic Classification Scheme
TGI: Target Group Index
TPI: Tax and Price Index
VTC: VAT Trade Classification

Bibliography: Statistical Sources

This bibliography lists the main statistical sources mentioned in the book. It is not intended as a comprehensive guide to sources and the directories and guides listed below should be used for further information. Sources of further reading are given in the final section of the bibliography.

General guides and directories

Catalogue of British Official Publications not Published by HMSO, 6 issues per year, Chadwyck-Healey
Directory of British Associations, annual, CBD Research
Directory of Business Information Sources, 1989, Macmillan
Directory of Salary Surveys, annual, Incomes Data Services
Government Statistics – a brief guide to sources, annual, CSO
Guide to Official Statistics, 1990, HMSO
Marketing Surveys Index, monthly, Marketing Strategies for Industry
National Salary Surveys, 1991, Remuneration Economics
Reviews of UK Statistical Sources, occasional, Chapman and Hall. (A series of individual titles on specific subjects with 25 titles published by the end of the 1980s.)
Sources of Unofficial UK Statistics, 1990, Gower
Statistical News, quarterly, HMSO

Statistics Users Conference Papers and Proceedings, annual, Statistics Users Council. (Each year the conference covers a particular subject area. The twentieth conference was held in November 1990.)

General statistics

Annual Abstract of Statistics, annual, HMSO
Digest of Welsh Statistics, annual, Welsh Office
Monthly Digest of Statistics, monthly, HMSO
Northern Ireland Annual Abstract of Statistics, annual, Department of Finance and Personnel
Regional Trends, annual, HMSO
Scottish Abstract of Statistics, annual, Scottish Office

Population statistics

Population census

The main published reports from the 1981 Census are listed below.

Census 1981: County Monitors, OPCS
Census 1981: County Reports, HMSO
Census 1981: Key Statistics for Local Authorities, Great Britain, HMSO
Census 1981: Key Statistics for Urban Areas, HMSO
Census 1981: National Report, Great Britain, 2 volumes, HMSO
Census 1981: New Towns Report, England and Wales, 2 volumes, HMSO
Census 1981: New Towns, Scotland, 2 volumes, HMSO
Census 1981: Regional Bulletins, GRO, Scotland
Census 1981: Regional Reports, HMSO
Census 1981: Report for Wales, HMSO

Single-topic reports

Census 1981: Country of Birth, Great Britain, HMSO
Census 1981: Country of Birth, Scotland, HMSO
Census 1981: Economic Activity, Great Britain, HMSO
Census 1981: Economic Activity, Scotland, HMSO
Census 1981: Household and Family Composition, England and Wales, HMSO
Census 1981: Household and Family Composition, Scotland, HMSO

Census 1981: Housing and Households, England and Wales, HMSO
Census 1981: Housing and Households, Scotland, HMSO
Census 1981: Migration, Scotland, 4 volumes, HMSO
Census 1981: National Migration, Great Britain, 2 volumes, HMSO
Census 1981: Persons of Pensionable Age, Great Britain, HMSO
Census 1981: Qualified Manpower, Great Britain, HMSO
Census 1981: Regional Migration, England and Wales, 2 volumes, HMSO
Census 1981: Sex, Age and Marital Status, Great Britain, HMSO
Census 1981: Usual Residence, Great Britain, HMSO
Census 1981: Welsh Language in Wales, HMSO
Census 1981: Workplace and Transport to Work, England and Wales, HMSO
Census 1981: Workplace and Transport to Work, Scotland, HMSO

A series of *Census Guides,* with summary statistics and commentary, was produced in 1984/85:
Census Guide 1: Britain's Elderly Population, OPCS
Census Guide 2: Britain's Children, OPCS
Census Guide 3: Britain's Workforce, OPCS
Census Guide 4: Britain's Households, OPCS

Other population statistics

Four-Weekly Vital Statistics Return of the Registrar General, Scotland, monthly, GRO, Scotland
Key Population and Vital Statistics, England and Wales, annual, HMSO

OPCS Monitors are produced by OPCS and are designed for the quick release of population data. A list of the *Monitors* on specific subjects is given in Chapter 3. The general population *Monitors* are listed below:

OPCS Monitor PP1, Population Estimates for England and Wales, annual, OPCS
OPCS Monitor PP2, Population Projections for England and Wales, annual, OPCS
OPCS Monitor PP3, Sub-National Population Projections for England and Wales, annual, OPCS

Population Estimates, Scotland, annual, HMSO
Population Trends, quarterly, HMSO
Registrar General's Annual Report for Scotland, annual, GRO, Scotland
Registrar General's Weekly Return for England and Wales, weekly, OPCS

Socio-economic statistics

Official statistics

Family Spending, annual, HMSO
General Household Survey, annual, HMSO
Household Food Consumption and Expenditure (Report of the National Food Survey), annual, HMSO
Key Data, annual, HMSO
Social Trends, annual, HMSO

Non-official statistics

British Social Attitudes: the 199– Report, annual, Gower
British Public Opinion, regular, MORI
Daily Life in the 19—s, occasional, BBC
Demographic Profiles, regular, Unit for Retail Planning Information
Gallup Political and Economic Index, monthly, Dod's Publishing and Research Ltd
GB-Site, continuous, CACI Ltd
Leisure Futures, quarterly, Henley Centre
Local Government Comparative Statistics, annual, CIPFA
Local Government Trends, annual, CIPFA. (A list of CIPFA titles on specific subjects is given in Chapter 4.)
National Shoppers Survey, continuous, CMT Ltd
Political, Social and Economic Review, quarterly, NOP
Town Focus/Town Focus Plus, continuous, Property Intelligence plc

Economic and financial statistics

Official statistics

Autumn Statement, annual, HMSO
CSO Business Bulletins, various titles, regular, CSO (Newport). Titles include:

Acquisitions and Mergers, quarterly
Capital Expenditure and Stock Building, quarterly
Company Finance, annual
Company Liquidity Survey, quarterly
Computing Services Industry, quarterly and annual

Credit Business, monthly
Cross Border Acquisitions and Mergers, quarterly
Currency of Invoicing, annual
Distributive and Service Trades, annual
Engineering Index of Production, monthly
Engineering Sales and Orders, monthly
Finance of Top Companies, twice a year
Insurance and Pensions, quarterly and annual
Machine Tools, monthly
Methodological Issues re Trade Statistics, bi-annual and occasional
Overseas Direct Investments and Earnings, annual
Overseas Earnings from Royalties, annual
Overseas Earnings of the Film and TV Industry, annual
Profitability (International), annual and occasional
Profitability of UK Companies, annual
Research and Development Statistics, annual
Statistical Changes in 1992, bi-annual and occasional
Steel Stocks, quarterly
UK Cinema Exhibitors, quarterly
Size Analyses of UK Businesses, annual

CSO Databank, regular updates, CSO
CSO Press Releases give the earliest information on economic trends and a list of these is given in Chapter 5.
CSO Statcall, continuous, CSO
Economic Briefing, 3 issues a year, HMSO
Economic Trends, monthly, HMSO
Economic Trends, Annual Supplement, annual, HMSO
Financial Statement and Budget Report, annual, HMSO
Financial Statistics, monthly, HMSO
Financial Statistics, Explanatory Handbook, annual, HMSO
Forecasts for the UK Economy: a comparison of independent forecasts, monthly, HM Treasury
Scottish Economic Bulletin, 6 issues a year, HMSO
Statistical Bulletins, regular, Scottish Office
Treasury Bulletin, quarterly, HMSO
UK Balance of Payments, 'CSO Pink Book', annual, HMSO
UK National Accounts, 'CSO Blue Book', annual, HMSO
UK National Accounts, Sources and Methods, occasional, HMSO
Welsh Economic Trends, annual, Welsh Office

Non-official statistics

Bank of England Quarterly Bulletin, quarterly, Bank of England. (The Bank of England also publishes various *Press Releases* and a list of these is given in Chapter 5.)
British Chambers of Commerce Quarterly Economic Survey, quarterly, Association of British Chambers of Commerce
Cityservice, continuous, British Telecom
Citywatch, continuous, Reuters
Cost of Living Report – regional comparisons, three a year, Reward Group
DRI Europe/DRI – Current Economic Indicators/DRI European Forecast, regular updates, DRI Europe
Economic Report and Survey, quarterly, London Chamber of Commerce
Economic Situation Report, monthly, CBI
Finstat, regular updates, FT Business Information Research
FT Monthly Stock Indices, monthly, FT Business Research Centre
FT Stats Fiche, weekly, McCarthys
Press Release, monthly, British Bankers Association
Quality of Markets Monthly Fact Sheet, monthly, International Stock Exchange
Quality of Markets Quarterly Review, quarterly, International Stock Exchange
Quarterly FT Actuaries Indices, quarterly, FT Business Research Centre
Regional Trends Survey, quarterly, CBI/Business Strategies Ltd
Topic, continuous, International Stock Exchange

Business statistics

Official statistics

Advance Energy Statistics, monthly, Department of Energy
Agriculture in the UK, annual, HMSO
Agricultural Statistics UK, annual, HMSO
Annual Report of HM Customs and Excise, annual, HMSO
Annual Review of Agriculture, annual, HMSO
British Tourism Survey, annual, British Tourist Authority
Business Monitor:

Census of Production reports are published annually in the *Business Monitor PA* series and a list of the reports is given in Chapter 5

Statistics of manufacturers' sales of products are given in the *Business Monitor PAS* series on an annual basis, in the *Business*

Monitor PQ series on a quarterly basis, and monthly in the *Business Monitor PM* series. All the titles are listed below:

Production Monitors

Extraction of fuels

PQ1113	Coal mining
PQ1300	Extraction of mineral oil and natural gas
PAS1401/1402	Mineral oil refining, lubricating oil and greases

Extraction of minerals and ores other than fuels:

Manufacture of metals and mineral products and chemicals

PAS2234	Steel wire and steel wire products
PAS2245	Aluminium and aluminium alloys
PAS2246	Copper, brass and other copper alloys
PAS2247	Miscellaneous non-ferrous metals and their alloys
PAS2310/2450	Extraction of stone, clay, sand and gravel working of stone and miscellaneous non-metallic minerals
PQ2330/2396	Salt and miscellaneous minerals
PAS2410	Structural clay products
PAS2420	Cement, lime and plaster
PQ2437	Miscellaneous building products of concrete, cement or plaster
PAS2440	Asbestos
PAS2460	Abrasives
PAS2471	Flat glass
PQ2478/2479	Glass containers and miscellaneous glass products
PAS2481	Refractory goods
PAS2489	Ceramic goods
PQ2511	Inorganic chemicals (except industrial gases)
PQ2512	Basic organic chemicals (except specialized pharmaceutical chemicals)
PAS2513	Fertilizers
PAS2514/2515	Synthetic resins, plastics materials and synthetic rubber
PAS2516	Dyestuffs and pigments
PQ2551	Paints, varnishes and painters' fillings

PAS2552	Printing ink
PAS2562/2569	Formulated adhesives, sealants and adhesive film, cloth and coil
PAS2563/2564	Chemical treatment of oils, fats and essential oils and flavouring materials
PQ2567	Miscellaneous chemical products for industrial use
PAS2568	Formulated pesticides
PQ2570	Pharmaceutical products
PAS2581	Soap and synthetic detergents
PAS2582	Perfumes, cosmetics and toilet preparations
PAS2591/2599	Photographic materials, chemicals and polishes and miscellaneous specialized products mainly for household and office use
PAS2600	Production of man-made fibres

Metal goods, engineering and vehicle industries

PAS3111	Iron castings
PAS3112	Non-ferrous metal foundries
PAS3120	Forging, pressing and stamping
PAS3137	Bolts, nuts, washers, rivets, springs and non-precision chains
PAS3138	Heat and surface treatment of metals (including sintering)
PAS3142	Metal doors, windows, etc
PAS3161	Hand tools and implements
PAS3162	Cutlery, spoons, forks and similar tableware; razors
PAS3163/3164	Metal storage vessels (mainly non-industrial) and packaging products of metal
PAS3165	Domestic heating and cooking appliances (non-electrical)
PAS3166	Metal furniture and safes
PAS3167	Domestic utensils of metal
PAS3169	Miscellaneous finished metal products
PAS3204	Fabricated constructional steelwork
PAS3205	Boilers and process plant fabrications
PAS3211	Agricultural machinery
PAS3212	Wheeled tractors
PQ3221	Metal-working machine tools

PAS3222	Engineers' small tools
PAS3230	Textile machinery
PAS3244	Food, drink and tobacco processing machinery; packaging and bottling machinery
PAS3245	Chemical industry machinery; furnaces and kilns; gas, water and waste treatment plant
PAS3251	Mining machinery
PAS3254	Construction and earth-moving equipment
PAS3255	Mechanical lifting and handling equipment
PAS3261/3262	Precision chains, other mechanical power transmission equipment, ball, needle and roller bearings
PQ3275	Machinery for working wood, rubber, plastics, leather and making paper, glass, bricks, and similar materials; laundry and dry cleaning machinery
PAS3276	Printing, bookbinding and paper goods machinery
PAS3281	Industrial (including marine) engines
PAS3283	Compressors and fluid power equipment
PAS3284	Refrigerating, space heating, ventilating and air-conditioning equipment
PAS3285	Scales, weighing machinery and portable power tools
PAS3286	Miscellaneous industrial and commercial machinery
PAS3287	Pumps
PAS3288	Industrial valves
PAS3289	Miscellaneous mechanical, marine and precision engineering
PAS3290	Ordnance, small arms and ammunition
PAS3301	Office machinery
PQ3302	Electronic data processing equipment
PAS3410	Insulated wires and cables
PAS3420	Basic electrical equipment
PAS3432	Batteries
PAS3433	Alarms and signalling equipment
PQ3434	Electrical equipment for motor vehicles cycles and aircraft

PAS3435	Miscellaneous electrical equipment for industrial use
PAS3441	Telegraph and telephone equipment
PQ3442	Electrical instruments and control systems
PAS3443	Radio and electronic capital goods
PQ3444	Components other than active components, mainly for electronic equipment
PAS3452	Gramophone records and pre-recorded tapes
PQ3453	Electronic sub-assemblies and active components
PAS3454	Electronic consumer goods and miscellaneous equipment
PAS3460	Domestic electric appliances
PAS3470	Electric lamps and lighting equipment
PQ3510	Motor vehicles and their engines
PAS3521	Motor vehicle bodies
PAS3522/3523	Trailers, semi-trailers and caravans
PQ3530	Motor vehicle parts
PQ3610	Shipbuilding and repairing
PAS3620	Railway and tramway vehicles
PAS3633/3634/3650	Motorcycles, cycles and miscellaneous vehicles
PAS3640	Aerospace equipment manufacturing and repairing
PAS3710	Measuring, checking and precision instruments and apparatus
PAS3720	Medical and surgical equipment and orthopaedic appliances
PAS3731/3732	Spectacles, unmounted lenses and optical precision instruments
PAS3733	Photographic and cinematographic equipment
PAS3740	Clocks, watches and other timing devices

Other manufacturing industries

PAS4115	Margarine and compound cooking fats
PAS4116	Organic oils and fats
PQ4122	Bacon curing and meat products
PAS4123	Poultry and poultry products
PAS4126	Animal by-products
PAS4147	Fruit and vegetable products

PAS4150	Fish products
PAS4180	Starch
PAS4196	Bread, flour and confectionery
PAS4197	Biscuits and crispbread
PQ4213	Ice-cream
PAS4239	Miscellaneous foods
PAS4240	Spirit distilling and compounding
PAS4261	Wines cider and perry
PAS4270	Brewing and malting
PQ4283	Soft drinks
PAS4290	Tobacco
PAS4310	Woollen and worsted
PAS4321/4336	Spinning and doubling of cotton, throwing, texturing etc of continuous filament yarn
PAS4322	Weaving of cotton, silk and man-made fibres
PAS4340	Spinning and weaving of flax, hemp and ramie
PAS4350	Jute and polypropylene yarns and fabrics
PQ4363	Hosiery and other weft knitted goods
PQ4364	Warp knitted goods
PAS4370	Textile finishing
PQ4384/4385	Carpets and other textile floor coverings
PAS4395	Lace
PAS4396	Rope, twine and net
PQ4398	Narrow fabrics
PQ4399	Miscellaneous textiles
PAS4410/4420	Leather and fellmongery and leather goods
PQ4510	Footwear
PQ4531	Weatherproof outerwear
PQ4532	Men's and boys' tailored outerwear
PQ4533	Women's and girls' tailored outerwear
PQ4534	Work clothing and men's and boys' jeans
PQ4535	Men's and boys' shirts, underwear and nightwear
PQ4536	Women's and girls' light outerwear, lingerie and infants' wear
PAS4537	Hats, caps and millinery
PQ4538	Gloves
PQ4539	Miscellaneous dress industries
PAS4555	Soft furnishings

PQ4556	Canvas goods, sacks and miscellaneous made-up textiles
PQ4557	Household textiles
PAS4560	Fur goods
PAS4610	Sawmilling, planing etc. of wood
PAS4620	Semi-finished wood products; preservation and treatment of wood
PAS4630	Builders' carpentry and joinery
PAS4640/4650	Wooden containers, miscellaneous wooden articles
PAS4663/4664	Articles of cork and plaiting materials, brushes and brooms
PAS4671	Wooden and upholstered furniture
PAS4672	Shop and office fitting
PAS4710	Pulp, paper and board
PAS4721	Wallcoverings
PAS4722	Household and personal hygiene paper products
PAS4723	Stationery
PAS4724	Packaging products of paper and pulp
PAS4725/4728	Packaging products of board and miscellaneous paper and board products
PAS4751	Printing and publishing of newspapers
PAS4752	Printing and publishing of periodicals
PAS4753	Printing and publishing of books
PAS4754	Miscellaneous printing and publishing
PAS4811/4820	Rubber tyres and inner tubes, retreading and specialist repairing of rubber tyres
PAS4812	Miscellaneous rubber products
PAS4831/4833	Plastic-coated textile fabrics and plastics floor coverings
PAS4832	Plastics semi-manufactures
PAS4834	Plastics building products
PAS4835	Plastics packaging products
PAS4836	Miscellaneous plastics products
PAS4910	Jewellery and coins
PAS4920	Musical instruments
PAS4941	Toys and games
PAS4942	Sports goods
PAS4954	Miscellaneous stationers' goods
PAS4959	Miscellaneous manufacturing industries

Monthly Production Monitor
PM3510 Car and commercial vehicle production

Business Monitor MA 21 Guide to the Classification of Overseas Trade Statistics, annual, HMSO
Business Monitor MM 20/MA 20 Overseas Trade Statistics of the UK, monthly and annual, HMSO
Business Monitor MQ 10 Overseas Trade Analysed in terms of Industries, quarterly, HMSO
Business Monitor PA 1003 Size Analysis of UK Businesses, annual, HMSO
Business Monitor PO 1000 Index of Commodities and Business Monitor Titles, 1991, HMSO
Business Monitor SDA 25 Retailing, annual, HMSO
Business Monitor SDA 26 Wholesaling, annual, HMSO
Business Monitor SDA 29 Services, annual, HMSO
Construction Forecasts, twice a year, Joint Forecasting Committee of the NEDC Construction Industry Sector Group (NEDO)
Digest of UK Energy Statistics, annual, HMSO
DoE Press Notices, regular, DoE
Economic Report on Scottish Agriculture, annual, Scottish Office
Energy Trends, monthly, Department of Energy
Housing and Construction Statistics annual and quarterly, HMSO
Indexes to the Standard Industrial Classification Revised 1980, HMSO
Industrial Economic Indicators Database, continuous, Business and Trade Statistics Ltd
Monthly Review of External Trade Statistics, monthly, DTI
Purchase Inquiry (Business Monitor PO 1008), 1984, HMSO
Standard Industrial Classification Revised 1980, HMSO
Transport Bulletins, regular, Department of Transport
Transport Statistics Great Britain, annual, HMSO
UK External Trade: area commodity analysis, regular, HMSO
Welsh Agricultural Statistics, annual, Welsh Office

Non-official statistics

A to Z of UK Marketing Data, regular, Euromonitor
Business Expectations Survey, quarterly, Dun & Bradstreet
CBI/Coopers Deloitte Survey of the Financial Services Sector, quarterly, CBI
CBI/FT Distributive Trades Survey, quarterly, CBI
CBI Industrial Trends Survey, quarterly, CBI
CBI Monthly Enquiry, monthly, CBI
Consumer and Economic Trends, quarterly, Projection 2000

Database Statistics, continuous, Market Location
Duns Marketing Database, continuous, Dun & Bradstreet
European Marketing Data and Statistics, annual, Euromonitor
Industrial Performance Analysis, annual, ICC
Key Business Ratios: guide to British business performance, annual, Dun & Bradstreet
Market Analysis and Information Database, regular, Maid Systems
Market Forecasts/ Growth Markets/ Top 400 Markets, annual, Market Assessment
Planning Consumer Markets, quarterly, Henley Centre
Poll of Members' Opinions, 6 times a year, Institute of Directors
Quoted UK, annual, Hoare Govett
Retail Business, monthly and quarterly, Economist Intelligence Unit

Labour statistics

Official statistics

Department of Employment Press Releases, monthly, Department of Employment
Employment Gazette, monthly, HMSO
Labour Costs Survey, annual, Department of Employment
Labour Force Survey, annual, HMSO
Labour Market Quarterly Report, quarterly, Department of Employment, Skills and Enterprise Network
National On-line Manpower Information System (NOMIS), regular updates, Durham University
New Earnings Survey, annual, HMSO
Standard Occupational Classification (SOC) 1991, HMSO
Survey of Personal Incomes, annual, HMSO
Training Statistics, annual, HMSO

Non-official statistics

Bargaining Report, monthly, Labour Research Department
Employment Affairs, 6 issues a year, CBI
Pay and Benefits Bulletin, monthly, IRS
Review of the Economy and Employment, regular, Institute of Employment Research, University of Warwick
Survey of Employment Prospects, quarterly, Manpower
Top Jobs Rewards Survey, annual, Remuneration Economics

Media and advertising data

Non-official statistics

Advertising Expenditure Forecasts, annual, Saatchi & Saatchi

Advertising Statistics Yearbook, annual, Advertising Association/NTC Publications

BARB Audience Surveys, weekly, Broadcasters' Audience Research Bureau

British Rate and Data (*BRAD*), monthly, BRAD

Cash and Carry Trade Report, annual, Nielsen

Cinema and Video Industry Audience Research (*CAVIAR*), annual, Cinema Advertising Association

CTN Trade Report, annual, Nielsen

Food Trade Report, annual, Nielsen

Forecast of Advertising Expenditure, quarterly, Advertising Association/NTC Publications

Homescan, continuous, Nielsen

JICNARS/RSL Marketing Data Book, annual, Research Services Ltd

Lifestyle Pocketbook, regular, NTC Publications

Lek-Trak/DIY-Trak, continuous, AGB

Marketing Pocketbook, annual, NTC Publications

Media Pocketbook, regular, NTC Publications

Media Register, monthly, Media Register

National Readership Survey, regular, Joint Industry Committee for National Readership Surveys

Nielsen Market Information Manual, annual, Nielsen

Nielsen Retail Index, continuous, Nielsen

Pharmacy and Drug Store Trade Report, annual, Nielsen

Quarterly Survey of Advertising Expenditure, quarterly, Advertising Association/NTC Publications

Regional Marketing Pocketbook, regular, NTC Publications

Target Group Index (TGI) annual, British Market Research Bureau

Television Consumer Audit, continuous, AGB

The 1990 Businessman's Survey, 1990, Business Media Research Committee

30 Year Readership Patterns of the NRS, annual, Guy Consterdine Associates

Tri-Media Digest of Brands and Advertisers, quarterly, Media Expenditure Analysis Ltd

General Bibliography

Allin, P. et al (1991), 'Labour market statistics for the 1990s', *Employment Gazette*, March, 135–38

Benjamin, B. (1989), *Population Statistics – A review of UK sources*, Aldershot: Gower

Central Statistical Office (1989), *CSO Starts as New Government Department*, London: CSO

Central Statistical Office (1991), 'Improving economic statistics – the Chancellor's initiative', *Economic Trends*, **448** (February) 84–7

Central Statistical Office (1991), 'Statistical changes in 1992', *Statistical Bulletin*, **4** (February)

Coldicott, I. (1990), 'Norfolk's survey of County Council's attitudes towards mid-year estimates of population', *BURISA Journal*, December, 3–5

Department of Employment (1990), 'Measures of unemployment: the claimant count and the Labour Force Survey', *Employment Gazette*, October, 506–13

Fiddick, P. (1991), 'BARB, BARB, Black Sheep', *Guardian*, 24 June, 25,27

Fildes, R. and Chrissanthaki, T. (1988), 'Using macro-economic forecasts' in R. Fildes (ed.), *World Index of Economic Forecasts*, 3rd edn, Aldershot: Gower

Fleming, M. and Nellis, J. (1984), 'House prices in the UK: the problem of measurement', *National Westminster Bank Quarterly Review*, November, 43–52

Hakim, C. (1982), *Secondary Analysis in Social Research: a guide to data sources and methods with examples*, London: George, Allen & Unwin

Hibberd, J. (1990), 'Official statistics in the late 1980s', *Treasury Bulletin*, **1**, (1), 2–13

Hibbert, J. (1990), 'Public confidence in the integrity and validity of official statistics', *Journal of the Royal Statistical Society Series A*, **153**, (2), 123–50

HMSO (1966), *Government Statistical Services: 4th report of the Estimates Committee, Session 1966–1967*, London: HMSO

HMSO (1977), *A Guide to Census Reports 1801–1966*, London: HMSO

HMSO (1981), *Government Statistical Services*, Cmnd 8236, London: HMSO

HMSO (1988), *White Paper; 1991 Census of Population*, Cmnd 430, London: HMSO

HMSO (1989), *Government Economic Statistics, a Cabinet Office Scrutiny Report*, London: HMSO

Hoinville, G. and Smith, T.M.F. (1982), 'The Rayner Review of Government Statistical Services', *Journal of the Royal Statistical Society Series A*, **145**, (2), 195–207

Johnson, C. (1988), *Measuring the Economy: a guide to understanding official statistics*, London: Pelican

Key Note (1988), *Official Business Statistics*, Hampton: Key Note

Lawlor, J. (1990), 'Monthly unemployment statistics: maintaining a consistent series', *Employment Gazette*, December, 601–8

Mahon, B., and Pearce, D. (1991), 'The 1991 Census of Great Britain: plans for content and output', *Social Trends*, 13–21

Market Research Society (1989), 'Special issue on geo-demographics', *Journal of the Market Research Society*, January, 1–131

Mort, D. (1988), 'How to find UK local statistics', *Business Information Review*, **5**, (1), July, 3–10

Mower, B. (1978), 'Government statistical information', *Aslib Proceedings*, **30**, (9), September, 321–6

Rayner, D. (1980), *A Review of Government Statistical Services – report to the Prime Minister*, London: HMSO

Royal Statistical Society (1990), 'Official statistics: counting with confidence', *Journal of the Royal Statistical Society Series A*, **154**, (1), 23–44

Scott, D. (1987), 'Making the most of statistics', *Business Information Review*, **3**, (3), January, 14–23

Scott, D. (1987), 'UK economic forecasts: a comparative survey', *Business Information Review*, **4**, (2), October, 3–23

Siddall, L. (1984), *A Survey of United Kingdom Non-Official Statistical Sources and their Role in Business Information*, Coventry: University of Warwick

Taylor, D. (1986), 'Seventeen statistical sleights', *Unemployment Bulletin*, **20**, Summer

Wallis, K.F. and Whitley, J.D. (1991), 'Sources of error in forecasts and expectations: UK economic models', *Journal of Forecasting*, **1**, (3), May, 231–53

Wilsdon, M. (1990), 'Government statistics', *Market Research Society Newsletter*, April, 44–5

Worrall, L. (1990), 'Improving the quality of Database UK', *BURISA Journal*, June, 3–8

Index

ABCC, 85
Academic institutions, 26
Acorn, 63
Acronyms, 197–198
  for professional groups, 45
Administrative methodology, 5–6
Advertising, 154, 181–182
  data, 213
  expenditure, 162–171
Advertising Association, 171–172
Advertising Statistics Yearbook, 171
Advisory National Statistics Committee, 14
Agriculture, 102
Agriculture Statistics, 102
Alcohol, 130
All–Share Index, 83
Alternative economics indicators, 88–90
Association of British Chambers of Commerce, *see* ABCC
Association of Market Survey Organizations, 155
Attwood Consumer Panel, 155
Audience surveys, 154
Audit Bureau of Circulation, 172
Audits, retail, 153–154
Audits of Great Britain, 155
Autumn Statement, 79

Balance of payments, 71–72, 173–174
  Blue Book (CS0), 77–78
  Pink Book (CS0), 78
Bank of England, 81
  press releases, 81–83
  Quarterly, 81-82
BARB, 158–159
Bargaining Report, 149
Behavioural typing, 64
Bicycle Association of Great Britain, 130
Blue Book (CS0), 77–78
BMRC, 161–162
Boards, marketing, 124
BRAD, 172
BREMA, 130, 177–178
British Social Attitudes, 54–55
Broadcasters Audience Surveys, *see* BARB
Budgets, 78–79
Building Services Research & Information Association, 131, 179

Building societies, 82–83, 89–90
  see also Construction
Business, BMRC, 161–162
Business Expenditure Survey, 125
Business Monitor, 107–115, 179
Business statistics, 93–136
  acronyms in, 197–198
  addresses, publishers, 183–195
  census of production, 96–101
  currency of, 5
  interpretation of, 8–9
  libraries, 195–196
  methodology and, 5–7
  need for, 3
  non-official (list), 211–212; *see also under* Non-official statistics
  official (list), 204–211; *see also under* Official statistics
  publishing, 7–8; *see also* Published statistics
  semi-official, 123–124

Carpet market, 130
CAVIAR, 161
CBI, 84–85, 148–149
CBI Industrial Trends Survey, 124–125
Census, 30–33, 176, 200–201
  employment, 141–142
  output, 33–37
  production, 96–101
  topics, 32
    household, 32
    personal, 32
Central heating, 179
Central Statistical Office, 12–13, 15–16, 18, 20–21
Chartered Institute of Public Finance & Accounting, 55–56
Cinema Advertising Association (CAA), 161
Cinema & Video Industry Audience Research, *see* CAVIAR
Cityservice, 91
Citywatch, 91
Civil service, 12–14, 101–102
Classification schemes, 6–7
  neighbourhood identification, 63
  of occupations, 138
  socio-economic, 43–45
  VAT, 103
Commodity statistics, 107–123
Companies in . . . series, 104
Confectionery, 130
Confederation of British Industry, *see* CBI
Construction, *see* Building societies
  Housing and Construction Statistics, 102
Consumer panels, 153
CSO, 73, 78, 96
  Blue Book, 77–78
  CS0 Databank, 79–80, 90–91
  Pink Book, 78
  press releases, 75
  Statcall, 80
  Statfax, 80
Currency, of statistics, 5
Cyclical Indicators, 76

Daily Life in the . . ., 65
Databases, *see* Online databases
Datastar, 133
Datastream International, 91
Demographic Profiles, 65
Digest of UK Energy Statistics, 103
Directory of Occupational Titles (CODOT), 138
Distribution, 104
DRI databank, 90–91
DTI, 13–14
Dun & Bradstreet industrial data, 126–127

Earnings, 145–147
EC, 122–123, 180
Economic data, *see* Financial data
Economic research institutes, 26
Economic Trends, 76–77
Employment, 141–143
  and unemployment, 143–145
Employment Affairs, 149
Employment Gazette, 49, 139–140, 142, 145, 147
Energy, 103
Enumeration Districts (EDs), 35
EPOS, 153–154
Estimation, of population, 37–38
European advertising, 171

Eurostat, 140
Exotic food, 134
Expenditure, 47–49
Export, *see* Imports/exports

Family Expenditure Survey, 46–49
Family Spending, 47–48
FES, 176–177
Finance, 202–204
Financial data, 67–91
  alternative, 88–90
  CSO
    Blue Book, 77–78
    databank, 79–80
    Pink Book, 78
    Statcall, 80
    Statfax, 80
  Economic Trends, 76–77
  Financial Statistics, 77
  local, 88
  non-official, *see* Non-official statistics
  official, *see* Official statistics
  on-line, 90–91
  press releases, 74–76
Financial institutions, 25
Financial Statistics, 77
Financial Times, 83–84, 133
  Finstat, 91
Fixed Interest Index, 84
'Footsie', 84
Forecasts, Treasury, 78–79
Forecasting, organizations for, 85–87
Frozen foods, 179
FT Index, 83–84
FT Ordinary Share Index, 83–84
FT-SE 100 Share Index, 84

Gallup Poll, 58
  see also Opinion polls
GB-SITE, 63
GDP, 70, 76, 174–176
General Household Survey, 51–53
Geo-demographic services, 58–64
Geographical coverage, 6
Gold Mines Index, 84
Government Securities Index, 84
Government Statistical Service, 15
Government statistics, official, 11–21
  see also under Official statistics
Gross Domestic Product, *see* GDP
Guide to British Business Performance, 126

Harmonized Commodity Description & Coding System, *see* HS
Harvest service, 133
Hay Management Consultants, 148
Henley Centre, 66
HMSO, 18–20
Homescan, 157
Housing and Construction Statistics, 102
HS, 7, 115–119, 122

IMF, 85
Imports/exports, 71–72, 115–123, 179–180
Income groups, 44
Income surveys, 147–149
Incomes Data Services, 148–149
Industrial Performance Analysis, 126
Industrial Relations Services, 148–149
Industry statistics, 124–127
Institute of Directors, 125–126
Institute for Fiscal Studies (IFS), 89
Institute of Practitioners in Advertising, 154
International Labour Office, 143–145
Interpretation, of statistics, 8–9
I P Sharp databank, 91

Job centres, 144
Joint Industry Committee for National Readership surveys (JICNARS), 159–160, 172
Joint Industry Committee for Radio Audience Research (JICRAR), 160–161
Joint Industry Committee for Regional Press Readership (JICREG), 161
Joint Industry Committees, 155, 160–161, 172

Kompass, 126

Labour force data, 140–141
Labour Force Survey, 140–141, 180–181
Labour Market Quarterly Report, 147
Labour market statistics, 137–149, 212

earnings, 145–147
general, 139–147
labour force, 140–141
Labour Market Quarterly Report, 147
SOC, 138–139
unemployment/employment, 141–145
Labour Research Department, 149
Lawnmowers, 134
Lek-Trak, 156, 177
Leisure Futures, 66
Liverpool University forecasts, 87
Local authorities, 23–25
economic data, 88
Local government population data, 41–42

Machine-readable business statistics, 123
Macroeconomic Modelling Bureau, 87
MAFF, 50–51, 141
MAID database, 133
Manufacturing companies, 26, 133–135
Market Location, 127
Market research, 25, 131–133, 151–152, 154–157
ad hoc, 152
syndicated, 152–155
audience survey, 154
omnibus, 153
panels, 153
readership survey, 154
retail audit, 153–154
Marketing boards, 124
Marplan, *see* Opinion polls
MEAL, 162–171, 181–182
Media Expenditure Analysis Ltd, *see* MEAL
Media organizations, 25
Media Register, 163–171
Media statistics, 213
Methodology, for statistics, 5–7
MORI, 58
see also Opinion polls
Mosaic, 63

NACE system, 94
National Food Survey (NFS), 49–51, 176–177
National Institute of Economic Social Research, 87
National Shoppers' Survey (NSS), 64
NEDO, 123–124
Neighbourhood identification, 58–63
classification schemes, 63
New Earnings Survey, 145–146
Nielsen Retail Index, 156–157
NOMIS, 142
Non-official statistics, 202, 204, 211–213
definition of, 4
finance, 81–87
ABCC, 85
Bank of England, 81–83
CBI, 84–85
forecasting organizations, 85–87
Stock Exchange, 83–84
industry, 124–126
performance data, 126
structure, 126–127
labour market, 147–149
population data, 41–42
published, 21–28
academic institutions, 26
economic research institutes, 26
financial institutions, 25
information sources, 27–28
key organizations, 21–26
local authorities, 23–25
manufacturing institutions, 26
market research, 25
media organizations, 25
stockbrokers, 25–26
strength of, 26–27
trade associations, 22–23
trade journals, 26
socio-economic data, 54–64
British Social Attitudes, 54–55
CIPFA, 55
geo-demographic services, 58–65
opinion polls, 55–58

OECD, 85, 143
Official statistics, 202–212
business, 96–123
agriculture, 102
census of production, 96–101
construction, 102

distribution, 104
energy, 103
imports, *see* Imports/exports
machine readable, 123
retailing, 104–106
sales, 107–123
services, 107
transport, 103
VAT, 103–104
wholesaling, 106–107
definition, 4
census data, 29–41
financial data, 68–74
balance of payments, 71–72
GDP, 70
improvements, 72–74
problems with, 68–70
RPI, 70–71
published, 12–21
development, 12–14
organization, 15–18
services, 18–21
subject coverage, 14–15
socio-economic data, 45–53
FES, 46–49
GHS, 51–53
NFS, 49–51
Social Trends, 45–46
Office of Population Censuses & Surveys (OPCS), 29–42
the census and, 29–42
local government (non-official statistics), 41–42
yearly titles, 40
Omnibus surveys, 153
Online databases, 19–20, 63, 90–91, 123, 133, 142, 149, 163
Town Focus, 65
OPCS, 138–139
Opinion polls, 55–58
OSCAR, 161
Outdoor Site Classification & Audience Research, *see* OSCAR
Output of the Production Industries, 76

PA series, 97–100, 179
Pay and Benefits Bulletin, 149
Pay Databanks, 149
PAYE, 146
Performance data, industry, 126
Pergamon Financial Data Services, 133
Personal behavioural typing, 64
Pink Book (CSO), 78
Pinpoint, 63
Point of sale, 153–154
Poll of Members Opinions (IoD), 125–126
Population data, 29–42
census, 30–37; *see also under* Census
estimates, 37–38
projections, 39–40
Postcode Address File (PAF), 50, 140
PQ series, 107, 109
Press releases, 74–76
PRODCOM, 110–111
Production, census of, 96–101
Professional bodies, 148
Professional organizations, 23
Public Finance and Accounting (CIPFA), 23, 55–56
Published statistics, 11–28
non-official, *see* Non-official statistics
official, *see* Official statistics
Publishing, of statistics, 7–8
Purchase Inquiry, 104

Qualitative market research, 152
Quarterly Survey of Advertising Expenditure, 171
Quarterly Turnover Inquiries (QTI), 73

Rayner Review, 122, 141
Readership surveys, 154
JICNARS, 159–160
JICREG, 161
Real time information services, 91
Regional industry surveys, 125
Retail audits, 153–154
Retailing, 104–106
Retail Price Index, *see* RPI
Reviews of the Economy & Employment, 147–148
Reward Group surveys, 148
Royal Statistical Society, 15
RPI, 70–72
Advisory Committee, 71, 73
structure, 72

Salary surveys, 147–149

Sales, 107–115
'Samples of anonymized records' (SARs), 37
Sampling, 5–6
Self-employed, 144–145
Semi-official business statistics, 123–124
Service sector statistics, 104–107
  distribution, 104
  retailing, 104–106
  wholesale, 106–107
Small Area Statistics (SAS), 35–37
  local areas covered, 36
    'high levels', 36
    'low levels', 36
Social classes, 44–45
Social Trends, 45–46
Society of Motor Manufacturers & Traders, 131
Socio-Economic Classification of the Population, 7
Socio-economic data, 43–66, 176–177, 202
  classification scheme, 43–45
  daily life, 65
  demographic profiles 65
  Henley Centre, 66
  non-official, *see* Non-official statistics
  official, *see* Official statistics
  Town Focus, 65
Standard Industrial Classification, 7, 94–96
Standard International Trade Classification, 7
  titles, 116–118
Standard Occupational Classification, 7, 138–139
Statistics, *see* Business statistics
Stockbrokers, 25–26
Stock Exchange, 83–84
  databases, 91
    Cityservice, 91
    Citywatch, 91
Sunday Times/IFS Index, 89
Superprofile, 63
SUPERSITE, 63
Survey of Employment Statistics, 147
Survey of Personal Incomes, 146
Surveys, 5–6
  market, companies, 25
  professional bodies, 148
  see also specific types of
Syndicated market research, 152

Target Group Index, 157–158
Tax & Price Index, *see* TPI
Television Consumer Audit, 155–156
Tourism, 124
Town Focus, 65
TPI, 74–75
Trade associations, 22–23, 127–131
Trade journals, 136, 172
  publishers, 26
Transport, 103
Transport Statistics Great Britain, 103
Treasury Bulletin, 79
Treasury Forecasts, 78–79
Tri-Media Digest of Brands & Advertisers, 163

UBOs, 143–144, 181
UK published statistics, *see* Non-official, Official *and also* Published statistics
UK Statistics Act, 14
Unemployment, 143–145, 180–181
  and employment, 141–143
Unit for Retail Planning Information, 65
United Nations' Standard International Trade Classification, 7, 116–118

VAT, 75, 105–107, 123
  records, 103–104
  Trade Classification, 7, 94, 103
Video recorders, 177–179

WEFA Group databank, 91
Wholesaling, 106–107
Wines, 130